THE OFFICIAL RULES OF ICE HOCKEY

TRIUMPH
B O O K S
CHICAGO

Typographer: Dana Ausec
Front cover photo courtesy of USA Hockey, Inc.
Interior photography courtesy of USA Hockey, Inc.

For more information about ice hockey and ordering more copies of the *Official Rules of Ice Hockey*, contact:

USA Hockey, Inc.
1775 Bob Johnson Drive
Colorado Springs, CO 80906-4090
Telephone (719) 576-8724 Fax (719) 538-1160

Distributed to the trade by:

Triumph Books
542 South Dearborn Street
Suite 750
Chicago, Illinois 60605
Telephone (312) 939-3330 Fax (312) 663-3557

Printed in the United States of America

ISBN 1-57243-587-9

USA Hockey is the National Governing Body for the sport of ice hockey in the United States.

Contents

PREFACE

Points of Emphasis
Philosophy of Youth Hockey
Codes of Conduct
Zero Tolerance Policy
Note to Reader

Points of Emphasis 2005 Through 2007 Seasons

The goal of USA Hockey is to promote a safe and positive playing environment for all participants while continuing to focus on skill development and enjoyment of the sport. To that end, all officials, coaches, players, parents, spectators and volunteers will comply with the following "Points of Emphasis" when participating in the sport of ice hockey.

Fair Play and Respect

Fair play and respect are the backbone of any successful amateur sports program. In order for a positive environment to be created, it is imperative that all participants and spectators have respect for all players, coaches, officials and the sport of hockey. Hockey is a game demanding high levels of concentration and skill.

As a player, it is necessary to play the game fairly, with respect for opponents and officials.

As a coach, it is necessary to instruct players during games and practices, ensuring that each player receives the training necessary to understand and play by the rules.

Officials should be diligent and confident when officiating the sport. Each official should enforce the playing rules fairly and respectfully.

All spectators are encouraged to support their teams while showing respect for all players, coaches, officials and other spectators.

Intimidation

Intimidation or "bullying" has no place in ice hockey. Any act that includes taunting or teasing or hazing of players, coaches, officials, or spectators by means of verbal ridicule, threat of physical violence, or physical violence itself will not be tolerated at USA Hockey events.

Coaches are responsible for instructing their players to play the sport in a safe and sportsmanlike manner. To that end, coaches are directed to teach only those skills necessary to allow for proper and legal body contact.

Players are encouraged to develop a deep sense of respect for all (opponents and officials) while endeavoring to enjoy the sport and improve their playing ability. Each player is encouraged to develop a sense of right and wrong when engaging in any type of body contact.

Stick Infractions

USA Hockey is continuing to place special emphasis on eliminating stick infractions from the game. Officials are directed to be aware of infractions such as high-sticking, slashing, hooking, cross-checking, spearing, and butt-ending and are encouraged to promptly and correctly assess the proper penalty.

Conclusion

With the goal of providing a safe and positive playing environment in mind, the Officiating and Coaching Education programs are directed to increase awareness among all officials and coaches with regard to these Points of Emphasis.

Philosophy of Youth Hockey

Enjoyment and recreational benefits are the major focus of new guidelines for youth hockey issued by the Board of Directors, USA Hockey. More than 80 percent of over 35,000 registered teams play in the age classifications 17-or-under, prompting the Youth Council of USA Hockey to emphasize the educational and recreational values of ice hockey.

USA Hockey recommended guidelines for youth hockey encourage a noncompetitive environment in which children and youth can learn the basic skills without the distractions that are often associated with an over-emphasis on winning. Mastery of the fundamental skills and the fun of playing are essential to the development of a lifelong interest in hockey. Programs must be conducted to accommodate the number of new players who wish to play hockey and to reduce the number who become disenchanted and drop out.

These voluntary guidelines are directed at children's programs, but they must be implemented by adults if they are to influence youth hockey programs. Coaches, officials, parents, administrators and rink operators must all do their part to ensure that the USA Hockey philosophy and the following guidelines are upheld:

Through Midget Age

- Team schedules should include at least two practices for every game.

- The recommended maximum number of games per season is: (A) 15 games for Mites, (B) 20 games for Squirts, (C) 30 games for Pee Wees, (D) 35 games for Bantams, and (E) 45 games for Midgets.

- Starting times for games should be no later than:
    Mites and Squirts-7:00 P.M.
    Pee Wees-8:00 P.M.
    Bantams-9:00 P.M.
    Midgets-10:00 P.M.
Any practice time scheduled before 3:00 P.M. should be set so that the earliest times are reserved for the older age classifications.

- Scoring records should be de-emphasized at the Mite, Squirt and Pee Wee classifications.

- Awards should be inexpensive and based on significant achievements. The most gratifying award any player can receive is the joy that comes from skill development that contributes to team success.

- An opportunity to practice and play under the direction of a good coach is the primary prerequisite to skill development. Players should be given ample opportunities to develop to the limits of their potential, regardless of their abilities.

- The recruitment of players, on a wide-spread geographic basis, for the establishment of Youth Division "elite teams," whose purpose is to win games and championships and to satisfy the personal self-interests of adults and organizations, is discouraged.

- It is recommended that adult volunteers place a primary emphasis on the formal education of players, and a de-emphasis on excessive competition and professionalism in the youth age classifications.

Codes of Conduct
Administrators Code of Conduct

- Follow the rules and regulations of USA Hockey and your association to ensure that the association's philosophy and objectives are enhanced.

- Support programs that train and educate players, coaches, parents, officials and volunteers.

- Promote and publicize your programs; seek out financial support when possible.

- Communicate with parents by holding parent/player orientation meetings as well as by being available to answer questions and address problems throughout the season.

- Work to provide programs that encompass fairness to the participants and promote fair play and sportsmanship.

- Recruit volunteers, including coaches, who demonstrate qualities conducive to being role models to the youths in our sport.

- Encourage coaches and officials to attend USA Hockey clinics and advise your board members of the necessity of these training sessions.

- Make every possible attempt to provide everyone, at all skill levels, with a place to play.

- Read and be familiar with the contents of the USA Hockey Annual Guide and Official Playing Rules.

- Develop other administrators to advance to positions in your association, perhaps even your own.

Coaches Code of Conduct

- Winning is a consideration, but not the only one, nor the most important one. You should care more about the child than winning the game. Remember, players are involved in hockey for fun and enjoyment.

- Be a positive role model to your players; display emotional maturity and be alert to the physical safety of players.

- Be generous with your praise when it is deserved; be consistent and honest; be fair and just; do not criticize players publicly; learn to be a more effective communicator and coach; don't yell at players.

- Adjust to the personal needs and problems of players; be a good listener; never verbally or physically abuse a player or official; give all players the opportunity to improve their skills, gain confidence and develop self-esteem; teach them the basics.

- Organize practices that are fun and challenging for your players. Familiarize yourself with the rules, techniques and strategies of hockey; encourage all your players to be team players.

- Maintain an open line of communication with your players' parents. Explain the goals and objectives of your association.

- Be concerned with the overall development of your players. Stress good health habits and clean living.

- To play the game is great; to love the game is greater.

On-Ice Officials Code of Conduct

- Act in a professional and businesslike manner at all times and take your role seriously.

- Strive to provide a safe and sportsmanlike environment in which players can properly display their hockey skills.

- Know all playing rules, their interpretations and their proper application.

- Remember that officials are teachers. Set a good example.

- Make your calls with quiet confidence, never with arrogance.

- Control games only to the extent that is necessary to provide a positive and safe experience for all participants.

- Violence should never be tolerated.

- Be fair and impartial at all times.

- Answer all reasonable questions and requests.

- Adopt a "zero tolerance" attitude toward verbal or physical abuse.

- Never use foul or vulgar language when speaking with a player, coach or parent.

- Use honesty and integrity when answering questions.

- Admit your mistakes when you make them.

- Never openly criticize a coach, player or other official.

- Keep your emotions under control.

- Use only USA Hockey–approved officiating techniques and policies.

- Maintain your health through a physical conditioning program.

- Dedicate yourself to personal improvement and maintenance of your officiating skills.

- Respect your supervisor and his/her critique of your performance.

Parents Code of Conduct

- Do not force your children to participate in sports, but support their desire to play their chosen sport. Children are involved in organized sports for their enjoyment. Make it fun.

- Encourage your child to play by the rules. Remember, children learn best by example, so applaud the good plays of both teams.

- Do not embarrass your child by yelling at players, coaches or officials. Showing a positive attitude toward the game and all of its participants will benefit your child.

- Emphasize skill development and practices and how they benefit your young athlete. De-emphasize games and competition in the lower age groups.

- Know and study the rules of the game, and support the officials on and off the ice. This approach will help develop and support the game. Any criticism of the officials only hurts the game.

- Applaud good efforts in both victory and defeat, and enforce the positive points of the game. Never yell or physically abuse your child after a game or practice—it is destructive. Work toward removing the physical and verbal abuse in youth sports.

- Recognize the importance of volunteer coaches. They are important to the development of your child and the sport. Communicate with them and support them.

- If you enjoy the game, learn all you can about hockey—and volunteer.

Players Code of Conduct

- Play for fun.
- Work hard to improve your skills.
- Be a team player; get along with your teammates.
- Learn teamwork, sportsmanship and discipline.
- Be on time for practices and games.
- Learn the rules and play by them. Always be a good sport.
- Respect your coach, your teammates, your parents, your opponents and the officials.
- Never argue with an official's decision.

Spectators Code of Conduct

- Display good sportsmanship. Always respect players, coaches and officials.

- Act appropriately; do not taunt or disturb other fans; enjoy the game together.

- Cheer good plays made by all participants; avoid booing opponents.

- Cheer in a positive manner and encourage fair play; profanity and objectionable cheers or gestures are offensive.

- Help provide a safe and fun environment; throwing any items on the ice surface can cause injury to players or officials.

- Do not lean over or pound on the glass; the glass surrounding the ice surface is part of the playing area.

- Support the referees and coaches by trusting their judgment and integrity.

- Be responsible for your own safety; be alert in order to prevent accidents caused by flying pucks and other avoidable situations.

- Respect locker rooms as private areas for players, coaches and officials.

- Be supportive after the game—win or lose. Recognize good effort, teamwork and sportsmanship.

Zero Tolerance Policy

In an effort to make ice and inline hockey more desirable and rewarding experiences for all participants, the USA Hockey Youth, Junior and Adult Councils and the InLine Section have instructed the Officiating Program to adhere to certain points of emphasis relating to sportsmanship. This campaign is designed to require all players, coaches, officials, parents/spectators and team officials and administrators to maintain a sportsmanlike and educational atmosphere before, during and after all USA Hockey–sanctioned games.

Thus, the following points of emphasis must be implemented by all Referees and Linesmen:

Players

A penalty (Zero Tolerance) shall be assessed whenever a player (please refer to Rule 601 for appropriate penalty):

1. Openly disputes or argues any decision by an official.

2. Uses obscene or vulgar language at any time, including any swearing, even if it is not directed at a particular person.

3. Visually demonstrates any sign of dissatisfaction with an official's decision.

Any time that a player persists in any of these actions, additional penalties shall be assessed per the penalty progression established under Rule 601.

Coaches

A minor penalty for unsportsmanlike conduct (Zero Tolerance) shall be assessed whenever a coach:

1. Openly disputes or argues any decision by an official.

2. Uses obscene or vulgar language in a boisterous manner to anyone at any time.

3. Visually displays any sign of dissatisfaction with an official's decision including standing on the boards or standing in the bench doorway with the intent of inciting the officials, players or spectators.

Any time that a coach persists in any of these actions, they shall be assessed a game misconduct penalty.

Officials

Officials are required to conduct themselves in a businesslike, sportsmanlike, impartial and constructive manner at all times. The actions of an official must be above reproach. Actions such as "baiting" or inciting players or coaches are strictly prohibited.

Officials are ambassadors of the game and must always conduct themselves with this responsibility in mind.

Parents/Spectators

The game will be stopped by game officials when parents/spectators displaying inappropriate and disruptive behavior interfere with other spectators or the game. The game officials will identify violators to the coaches for the purpose of removing parents/spectators from the spectator's viewing and game area. Once removed, play will resume. Lost time will not be replaced and violators may be subject to further disciplinary action by the local governing body. This inappropriate and disruptive behavior shall include:

1. Use of obscene or vulgar language in a boisterous manner to anyone at any time.

2. Taunting of players, coaches, officials or other spectators by means of baiting, ridiculing, threat of physical violence or physical violence.

3. Throwing of any object in the spectators viewing area, players bench, penalty box or on ice surface, directed in any manner as to create a safety hazard.

Note to Reader

Please note that the shaded text within this edition of the Official Rules signifies an adjustment within that particular text. Additionally, the words "he," "him" and "his" are used to include both male and female participants.

SECTION ONE
THE RINK

Rule 101 Rink

(a) The game of "Ice Hockey" shall be played on an ice surface known as a "RINK."

Rule 102 Dimensions of Rink

(a) As nearly as possible, the dimensions of the rink shall be 200 feet long and 100 feet wide. In all ice rinks used for invitational tournaments and regional Playoffs and national championships the ice surface dimensions shall be not less than 185 feet by 85 feet.

The rink shall be surrounded by a wooden or fiberglass wall or fence, known as the "BOARDS," which shall extend not less than 40 inches and not more than 48 inches above the level of the ice surface. The ideal height of the boards above the ice surface shall be 42 inches. It is recommended that the kickplate at the bottom of the boards be yellow.

The corners shall be uniformly rounded in the arc of a circle with a radius of 23 feet minimum to 28 feet maximum.

(Note) USA Hockey recommends that for new or refurbished construction, refer to the ASTM Standard Guide for Ice Hockey Playing Facilities (F 1703-04).

(b) The boards shall be constructed in such a manner that the surface facing the ice shall be smooth and free of any obstruction or any object that could cause injury to players.

All doors giving access to the playing surface must swing away from the ice surface.

It is recommended that the entire rink, including players and penalty benches, be enclosed by protective safety glass, wire and/or other protective screens of sufficient height designed to separate players from spectators. All gear used to hold such protective equipment in place shall be mounted on the boards on the side away from the playing surface.

Rule 103 Goal Posts and Nets

(a) Thirteen feet from each end of the rink and in the center of a red line two inches wide drawn completely across the width of the ice and continuing vertically up the side of the boards, regulation goal posts and nets shall be set in such a manner as to remain stationary during the progress of a game. If applicable, the goal posts shall be anchored in such a manner as to permit a goal post to be dislodged when hit by a degree of force such as would be provided by a player sliding into or being checked into it.

If the distance from the end of the rink to the goal line is not 13 feet, it must be a minimum of 12 feet and a maximum of 15 feet.

(b)   The goal posts shall be of approved design and material, extending vertically four feet above the surface of the ice and set six feet apart measured from the inside of the posts. A cross bar of the same material as the goal posts shall extend from the top of one post to the top of the other. It is recommended that the goal frames do not have a metal deflector plate along the base of the back of the goal frame.

(c)   There shall be attached to each goal frame a net of approved design.

(d)   The goal posts and cross bars shall be painted in red and all other exterior surfaces shall be painted in white.

(e)   The red line, two inches wide, between the goal posts on the ice and extended completely across the rink, shall be known as the "GOAL LINE."

(f)   The Goal area, enclosed by the goal line and the base of the goal, shall be painted white.

Rule 104   Goal Crease and Goalkeeper's Privileged Area

(a)   In front of each goal a "GOAL CREASE" area shall be marked by a red line two inches in width.

(b)   The goal crease shall be laid out as follows: A semi-circle six feet in radius and two inches in width shall be drawn using the center of the goal line as the center point. The goal crease area, excluding the red lines, shall be painted light blue in color. It is recommended that there shall be two "L-shaped" red markings in each goal crease. Each line shall be five inches long and two inches wide. The corners shall touch the goal crease line four feet out from the goal line. The lines shall be both parallel and perpendicular to the goal line.

(c)   The goal crease area shall include all the space outlined by the semi-circular crease lines (including crease lines) and extending vertically to the level of the top of the goal frame.

(d)   The goalkeeper's "PRIVILEGED AREA" is an area bounded in the rear by the end boards, in front by an imaginary line connecting the end zone face-off spots and on the sides by imaginary lines extending perpendicular from the end boards to the end zone face-off spots. (For the goalkeeper's privileges within this area, see Rules 606(b) Note, Charging and 612(b), Falling on Puck.)

(e)   The goalkeepers may only take warm-ups in the Goalkeeper's Privileged Area extended to include the area formed by a line from each end zone face-off spot to where the goal line meets the side boards. (See Rink diagram.)

    For a violation of this rule, after a warning, the offending team shall be assessed a bench minor penalty.

Rule 105   Division of Ice Surface

(a)   The ice area between the two goals shall be divided into three parts by lines, 12 inches in width and blue in color, drawn 60 feet out from the goal lines and extended completely across the rink, parallel with the goal lines and continued vertically up the side of the boards. The 60 feet shall be measured from the edge of the goal line closest to the end boards to the furthest edge of the blue line.

(b)   That portion of the ice surface in which the goal is situated shall be called the "DEFENDING ZONE" of the team defending that goal; the central portion shall be known as the "NEUTRAL ZONE" and the portion farthest from the defended goal as the "ATTACKING ZONE." The zone line shall be considered part of the zone that the puck is in.

(c)   There shall also be a line, 12 inches in width and red in color, drawn completely across the rink in center ice, parallel with the goal lines and continued vertically up the side of the boards, known as the "CENTER LINE." This line shall contain at regular intervals markings of a uniform and distinctive design that will easily distinguish it from the two blue lines, the outer edges of which must be continuous.

Rule 106 Center Ice Spot and Circle

(a)   A circular blue spot, 12 inches in diameter, shall be marked exactly in the center of the rink; and with this spot as a center, a circle of 15 feet radius shall be marked with a blue line 2 inches in width. The width of this line shall be included in the radius.

Rule 107 Face-Off Spots in Neutral Zone

(a)   Two red spots two feet in diameter shall be marked on the ice in the Neutral Zone five feet from the near edge of the blue line. Within each face-off spot draw two parallel lines four inches from the top and bottom of the spot. The area within the two lines shall be painted red, the remainder shall be painted white. The spots shall each be 22 feet from the center of the ice surface.

Rule 108 End Zone Face-Off Spots and Circles

(a)   In both end zones and on both sides of each goal, red face-off spots and circles shall be marked on the ice. The face-off spots shall be two feet in diameter. Within each face-off spot draw two parallel lines four inches from the top and bottom of the spot. The area within the two lines shall be painted red, the remainder shall be painted white.

One foot away from the outer edges of the face-off spot, two lines shall be drawn parallel with the side boards that shall be four feet in length and 18 inches apart. Parallel to the end boards, commencing at the end of the line nearest to the face-off spot, a line shall extend 2 feet 10 inches in length. All lines shall be 2 inches in width.

The circles shall be 2 inches wide with a radius of 15 feet from the center of the face-off spots. The width of this line shall be included in the radius. On both sides of each end zone face-off circle shall be two lines 2 feet long, 2 inches wide and 4 feet apart.

(b)   The location of the face-off spots shall be fixed in the following manner: Along a line 20 feet from each goal line and parallel to it, mark two points 22 feet on both sides of the straight line joining the centers of the two goals. Each such point shall be the center of a face-off spot and circle.

Rule 109 Players' Bench

(a)   Each rink shall be provided with seats or benches for the use of players of both teams and the accommodations provided including benches and doors shall be uniform for both teams. Such seats or benches shall have accommodations for at least 14 persons of each team and shall be placed immediately alongside the ice, in the Neutral Zone, as near to the center of the rink as possible with doors opening in the Neutral Zone and convenient to the dressing rooms.

   Each players' bench should be 24 feet in length. The players' benches should be on the same side of the playing surface opposite the penalty bench and should be separated by a substantial distance. Where physically possible, each players' bench shall have two doors in the Neutral Zone and all doors opening to the playing surface shall be constructed so that they swing away from the ice surface.

(b)   None but players in uniform and Team Officials (up to a maximum of four) shall be permitted to occupy the bench area so provided.

(c)   There shall be no use of tobacco products or alcoholic beverages on the players' bench, penalty bench, timekeeping area or on the ice by any person. A team shall be warned by the Referee for the first offense by any player or Team Official during a game and, thereafter, a bench minor penalty shall be assessed for each such offense during the game.

Rule 110 Penalty Bench

(a)   Each rink must be provided with benches or seats to be known as the "PENALTY BENCH." It is preferable to have separate penalty benches for each team to be separated from each other and substantially separated from either players' bench. The penalty bench(es) must be situated in the Neutral Zone.

Nonpenalized players and goalkeepers are not permitted to occupy the penalty bench. For a violation of this rule, play shall not continue until removal of the offending person(s).

(b)   On the ice immediately in front of the Penalty Timekeeper's seat there shall be marked in red on the ice a semicircle of 10 feet radius and two inches in width that shall be known as the "REFEREE'S CREASE."

Rule 111 Signal and Timing Devices

(a)   Each rink shall be provided with a siren or other suitable sound device for the use of Timekeepers.

(b)   Each rink shall be provided with some form of electrical clock for the purpose of keeping the spectators, players and game officials accurately informed as to all time elements at all stages of the game, including the time remaining to be played in any period.

Time recording for both game time and penalty time shall show time remaining to be played or served.

(c)   Behind each goal electric lights shall be set up for the use of the Goal Judges. A red light will signal the scoring of a goal. Where automatic lights are available, a green light will signify the end of a period or a game.

(Note) A goal cannot be scored when a green light is showing.

The red light shall be connected to the timing device in such a manner so that when the period ends it will not be possible for the Goal Judge to turn it on. However, the fact that the Goal Judge may not be able to turn on the red light does not necessarily mean that no goal has been scored. The determining factor is whether or not the puck completely crosses the entire goal line before the period ends.

SECTION TWO
TEAMS

Rule 201 Composition of Teams

(a)   A team must start a game with six players on the ice. Any time that a team has been reduced to less than four players, the game shall be declared a forfeit. A maximum of 20 players, including goalkeepers, shall be permitted to play in a game.

The maximum number of players, excluding goalkeepers, shall not exceed 18.

(b)   Each team shall appoint and designate on the scoresheet a Head Coach prior to the start of the game. The Head Coach shall be in control of and responsible for the actions of all team personnel.

Rule 202 Captain of Team

(a)   One Captain and not more than two Alternates shall be appointed by each team. In each instance, only one of these designated players shall have the privilege of discussing with the Referee any questions relating to interpretation of rules that may arise during the progress of a game. They should wear the letter "C" or "A," approximately three inches in height and in contrasting color, in a conspicuous position on the front of the sweater.

(b)   The Referee and Official Scorer shall be advised prior to the start of each game, the name of the Captain of the team and the designated Alternate(s). This information will be added to the scoresheet.

(c)   No goalkeepers shall be entitled to exercise the privileges of Captain.

(d)   Any Captain or player who comes off the bench and makes any protest or intervention with the Officials for any purpose shall be assessed a minor penalty under Rule 601(a), Abuse of Officials.

A complaint about a penalty is NOT a matter "relating to the interpretation of the rules" and a minor penalty shall be imposed against any Captain or other player making such a complaint.

Rule 203 Players in Uniform

(a) At the beginning of each game the Manager or Coach of each team shall list the players and goalkeepers who shall be eligible to play in the game. This list shall be given to the Referee or Official Scorer and no change shall be permitted in the list or addition thereto shall be permitted after commencement of the game, except as permitted under Rule 203(b).

(b) However, if the Referee deems the omission as an inadvertent clerical error, a rostered player or goalkeeper may be added to the scoresheet during a stoppage of play after commencement of the game. The offending team shall be assessed a bench minor penalty for each such addition.

No roster deletions are permitted under this rule, and maximum roster size under Rule 201(a) shall limit the number of allowable additions.

(c) Each team shall be allowed one goalkeeper on the ice at one time. The goalkeeper may be removed and another player substituted. Such substitute shall not be permitted the privileges of the goalkeeper.

A goalkeeper may be substituted for by another goalkeeper during play with full goalkeeper privileges. However, once a goalkeeper has been replaced by a substitute goalkeeper, he may not return to play until the next stoppage of play. For a violation, a bench minor penalty shall be assessed for illegal substitution.

(d) Each player and each goalkeeper listed in the lineup of each team shall wear a visible individually identifying number at least 10 inches high on the back of his sweater. Only whole numbers 0 to 99, inclusive, are permitted.

The number may be eight inches in the Midget and Bantam classifications and six inches in height in the Squirt, Pee Wee and Mite classifications.

All players of each team shall be dressed uniformly.

(e) It is recommended that each team have on its bench a substitute goalkeeper who shall be fully dressed and equipped to play.

When the substitute goalkeeper enters the game he will take his position without delay and no warm-up shall be permitted, except when either team uses its Time-out under Rule 637(e).

(f) Except when the goalkeeper(s) is/are incapacitated, no player on the playing roster in that game shall be permitted to wear the equipment of the goalkeeper. If a team's goalkeeper(s) is/are unavailable to continue, a team must immediately appoint a temporary goalkeeper (see Glossary) or place an additional skater on the ice with none of the goalkeeper's privileges.

Rule 204 Playing Lineup

(a) Upon the Referee's signal prior to the start of a period and following any stoppage of play, the visiting team shall promptly place a lineup on the ice, ready for play and no substitution shall be made from that time until play has been resumed. The home team may then make any desired substitution that does not result in the delay of the game.

If there is any undue delay by either team in changing lines, the Referee shall order the offending team or teams to take their positions immediately and not permit line changes.

(Note) When a substitution has been made under the above rule, no additional substitution may be made until play commences except when any penalty is imposed.

Rule 205 Change of Players

(a) Players may be changed at any time from the players' bench, provided that the player or players leaving the ice shall always be at the players' bench and out of the play before any change is made.

If, in the course of making a substitution, either the player entering or leaving the game deliberately plays the puck with the stick, skates or hands, or checks or makes any physical contact with an opposing player while the retiring player is actually on the ice, then a bench minor penalty for "too many players on the ice" will be called.

(Note) If, in the course of a substitution, either the player entering the play or the player retiring is struck by the puck accidentally, the play will not be stopped and no penalty will be called.

(b) A goalkeeper may be changed for another player at any time under the conditions set out in this section.

(Note) When a goalkeeper leaves his goal area and proceeds to his players' bench for the purpose of substituting another player, the rear Linesman shall be responsible to see that the substitution made is not illegal by reason of the premature departure of the substitute from the bench (before the goalkeeper is at the bench and out of play). If the substitution is made prematurely, the Linesman shall stop the play immediately by blowing his whistle unless the nonoffending team has possession of the puck, in which event the stoppage will be delayed until the puck changes hands. There shall be no time penalty to the team making the premature substitution but the resulting face-off will take place on the center face-off spot. Where play has stopped with the puck in the offending team's defending half of the ice, the face-off shall take place at the point of the stoppage of play, unless otherwise covered in these rules.

(c) If there are less than two minutes remaining in either regulation time or anytime during overtime and a minor or bench minor penalty is imposed for deliberate illegal substitution, such as too many players on the ice or leaving the penalty bench too soon, a penalty shot/optional bench minor shall be awarded against the offending team in lieu of the minor or bench minor penalty.

(Note) The intent of this rule is to award a penalty shot/optional bench minor only when the extra player(s) are "deliberately" put on the ice. When a substitution error is made and there are too many players on the ice, the normal bench minor penalty shall be assessed regardless of the time remaining in the game.

(d) A player serving a penalty on the penalty bench, who is to be changed after the penalty has been served, must proceed at once by way of the ice and be at his own players' bench before any change can be made.

(e)   During a stoppage of play a goalkeeper may not go to his players' bench without the permission of the Referee unless he is substituted for by another player or goalkeeper. When a substitution for the goalkeeper has been made under this rule, the goalkeeper shall not resume his position until play resumes, except that he shall be permitted immediate re-entry into the game when any penalty is imposed.

(f)   For a violation of this rule a bench minor penalty shall be imposed unless otherwise provided in the Playing Rules.

Rule 206 Injured Players

(a)   When a player, other than a goalkeeper, is injured or compelled to leave the ice during a game, he may retire from the game and be replaced by a substitute, but play must continue without the teams leaving the ice.

(b)   If a goalkeeper sustains an injury or becomes ill he must be ready to resume play immediately or be replaced by a substitute goalkeeper. No additional time shall be allowed by the Referee for the purpose of enabling the injured or ill goalkeeper to resume his position. (See also Rule 205(e).)

(c)   The substitute goalkeeper shall be subject to the regular rules governing goalkeepers and shall be entitled to the same privileges.

(d)   If a penalized player has been injured he may proceed to the dressing room without the necessity of taking a seat on the penalty bench.

If the injured player receives a minor or major penalty, the penalized team shall place a substitute on the penalty bench immediately and no replacement for the penalized player shall be permitted to enter the game except from the penalty bench, provided that should the penalized player return to the game before his penalty has expired, he may replace the substitute player on the penalty bench during a stoppage of play.

The penalized player who has been injured and been replaced on the penalty bench shall not be eligible to play until his penalty has expired.

For a violation of this rule a bench minor penalty shall be imposed.

(Note) No substitution on the penalty bench is required under this rule for any player(s) who have been immediately substituted on the ice under Rule 402(f)-coincident minor penalties and/or Rule 403(c)-coincident major penalties.

(e)   When a player is injured so that he cannot continue play or go to his bench, the play shall not be stopped until the injured player's team has secured possession of the puck; if the player's team is in possession of the puck at the time of injury, play shall be stopped immediately, unless his team is in a scoring position.

(Note) In the case where it is obvious that a player has sustained a serious injury, the Referee and/or Linesman may stop the play immediately.

(f)   A player other than a goalkeeper, whose injury appears serious enough to warrant the stoppage of play, may not participate further in the game until the completion of the ensuing face-off.

(g)   A player or goalkeeper who is obviously bleeding shall be ruled off the ice immediately if observed during a stoppage of play. If observed during play, play shall be stopped immediately and the bleeding player or goalkeeper then ruled off the ice. Said player or goalkeeper shall not be allowed to return to play until the bleeding has been stopped and the cut or abrasion covered. It is required that any affected equipment/uniform be properly decontaminated or exchanged.

Likewise, if an on-ice official is bleeding, at the next stoppage, said official shall seek treatment to stop the bleeding and cover the cut or abrasion before continuing. It is required that any affected equipment/uniform be properly decontaminated or exchanged.

SECTION THREE
EQUIPMENT

Rule 301 | Sticks

(a) The sticks shall be made of wood or other material approved by the Rules Committee, and must not have any projections. Adhesive tape of any color may be wrapped around the stick at any place for the purpose of reinforcement or to improve control of the puck. The end of a hollow stick must be fully covered.

(b) No stick shall exceed 63 inches in length from the heel to the end of the shaft. The widened portion of the goalkeeper's stick extending up the shaft from the blade shall not extend more than 26 inches from the heel and shall not exceed 3½ inches in width.

   The blade of a player's stick shall not exceed 12½ inches from the heel to the end of the blade, nor shall the blade be more than 3 inches in width at any point nor less than 2 inches in width.

   The blade of the goalkeeper's stick shall not be less than 2 inches in width at any point nor shall the blade exceed 3½ inches in width at any point except at the heel, where it must not exceed 4½ inches in width, nor shall the goalkeeper's stick exceed 15½ inches in length from the heel to the end of the blade.

   All edges of the blade shall be beveled.

(c) The curvature of the blade of the stick shall be restricted in such a way that the distance of a perpendicular line measured from a straight line drawn from the base of the heel to the base of the toe to the point of maximum curvature shall not exceed ½ inch.

(d) A minor penalty shall be imposed on any player or goalkeeper who uses a stick not conforming to the provisions of this rule.

   (Note 1) When a formal complaint is made by the Captain of a team against the dimensions of any stick, the Referee shall make the necessary measurement immediately.

   If the complaint is not sustained, a bench minor penalty shall be imposed on the team requesting the measurement.

Equipment

(Note 2) A player who participates in the play while carrying a stick to his goalkeeper shall incur a minor penalty under this rule.

(Note 3) If a goal is scored with an illegal stick, the proper penalty shall be assessed and the goal shall be allowed.

(e)   A minor plus a misconduct penalty shall be imposed on any player who refuses to surrender his stick for measurement when requested to do so by the Referee.

(f)   A minor penalty shall be assessed to a player or goalkeeper who participates in the play while he is in possession of more than one stick, except that no penalty shall be assessed to a player who is accidentally struck by the puck while he is carrying a replacement stick to a teammate.

Rule 302   Skates

(a)   All players and On-Ice Officials must wear hockey skates of a design approved by the Rules Committee. All skates worn by players (but not goalkeepers) and by the On-Ice Officials shall be equipped with approved safety heel tips, if so designed.

When the Referee becomes aware that any player is wearing skates on which the protective heel tip is missing or broken, if so designed, he shall order that player off the ice immediately and such player shall not be permitted to participate further in the game until the heel tip has been replaced.

It is recommended that all players (except goalkeepers) and On-Ice Officials wear skates with blades that have been approved by HECC.

(b)   The use of speed skates or fancy skates or any skate so designed that it may cause injury is prohibited.

(c)   No additional equipment or contrivance shall be attached to the skates of any player or goalkeeper.

Rule 303 | Goalkeeper's Equipment

(a)   With the exception of skates and stick, all the equipment worn by the goalkeeper must be constructed solely for the purpose of protecting the head or body, and he must not wear any garment or use any contrivance that would give him undue assistance in keeping goal.

(Note) Cages on gloves and abdominal aprons extending down the front of the thighs on the outside of the pants are prohibited. "Cage" shall mean any lacing or webbing or other material in the goalkeeper's glove joining the thumb and index finger that is in excess of the minimum necessary to fill the gap when the goalkeeper's thumb and forefinger in the glove are fully extended and spread and includes any pocket or pouch effect produced by excess lacing or webbing or other material between the thumb and forefinger when fully extended or spread.

Protective padding attached to the back or forming part of goalkeeper's blocker glove shall not exceed 8 inches in width nor more than 16 inches in length at any point. The cuff of the goalkeeper's catching glove shall not exceed 8½ inches in width nor should the circumference of the glove exceed 48 inches. Any bar or attachment (cheater bar) between the cuff and the thumb shall only extend from the cuff to the thumb in a straight line. Any other pocket, pouch or contrivance added to the glove by a manufacturer or otherwise is not acceptable and makes the glove illegal.

(b)   The leg guards worn by goalkeepers shall not exceed 12 inches in extreme width when on the leg of the player.

(c)   It is compulsory for all goalkeepers to wear helmets and full facemasks. Throat/neck protectors are recommended. No form fitted facemasks shall be permitted.

(d)   A minor penalty shall be imposed on any goalkeeper using illegal equipment in a game. Any required measurement or other examination shall be conducted immediately.

Rule 304 Protective Equipment

(Note) Although some protective equipment is not mandatory in all age classifications, USA Hockey strongly recommends that all players and goalkeepers in all age classifications properly wear an internal mouthpiece, a HECC approved helmet and a HECC approved full facemask for all games and practices.

(a)   Each participant is personally responsible to wear protective equipment for all games, warm-ups and practices. Such equipment should include gloves, shin pads, shoulder pads, elbow pads, hip pads or padded hockey pants, protective cup, tendon pads plus all head protective equipment as required by USA Hockey rules. It is recommended that all protective equipment be designed specifically for ice hockey.

All protective equipment, except gloves, padded hockey pants, helmet/facemask and goalkeeper's leg guards, must be worn under the uniform. For violation of this rule after a warning by the Referee a minor penalty shall be imposed.

(Note) Players, including goalkeepers, violating this rule shall not be permitted to participate in the game until such equipment has been corrected or removed.

In all classifications, if the goalkeeper's helmet/facemask comes off during play, the Referee or Linesman shall stop play immediately.

In all classifications excluding Adults, if a player's helmet/facemask comes off during play, the Referee or Linesman shall stop play immediately. The player shall be ruled off the ice and may not participate in the game until completion of the ensuing face-off.

A minor penalty shall be assessed to a goalkeeper or player who causes a stoppage of play by deliberately removing his helmet/facemask during play.

In Adult classifications a player, excluding the goalkeeper, whose helmet/facemask has come off his head during play may not resume play until his helmet/facemask has been properly replaced. A player not conforming to this rule shall be assessed a minor penalty.

(b) It is compulsory for all players in all classifications to wear a hockey helmet, with helmet strap properly fastened. (See Rule 304(d) Note.)

It is mandatory that all players wear a HECC approved helmet (including ear protection) with the following exception:

Players in the Adult age classification must wear a hockey helmet (HECC approved or not) with helmet strap properly fastened.

All players on the players' and the penalty bench must wear the protective helmet/facemask while in the bench area. For a violation of this rule, after a warning by the Referee, a misconduct penalty shall be assessed to the offending player.

(c) All players, including goalkeepers, in the Pee Wee through Midget (including High School) and in the Girls/Women 8-or-under through 19-or-under age classifications are required to wear a colored (nonclear) internal mouthpiece that covers all the remaining teeth of one jaw, customarily the upper.

For the first violation of this rule, the team shall be issued a warning. A misconduct penalty shall be assessed to any player or goalkeeper of that team for a subsequent violation during that game.

It is recommended, in all classifications, that the mouthpiece be form fitted by a dentist.

(d) All players, including goalkeepers, in all age classifications below Adults, are required to wear a facemask certified by HECC, plus any chin protection that accompanies the facemask.

(Note) Any helmet or facemask that is altered except as permitted in Rule 304(b) shall be deemed to be illegal equipment and shall not be allowed to be used in a game. (This shall include helmets from which a part has been cut or removed, facemasks from which the chin-cup has been removed or any other such alterations from the original manufacturing specifications.)

(e) All players must wear the required protective equipment in the manner for which it is designed. For violation of this rule a misconduct penalty shall be imposed.

Rule 305 Dangerous Equipment

(a) The use of pads or protectors made of metal, or of any other material likely to cause injury to a player, is prohibited.

The wearing of casts or splints made of hard or unyielding materials is prohibited, even if padded, unless directed in writing by a licensed medical physician. Such casts or splints must be covered on all exterior surfaces with no less than ½-inch thick, high-density, closed-cell polyurethane or an alternate material of the same minimum thickness and similar physical properties to protect an injury.

(b) A glove from which all or part of the palm has been removed or cut to permit the use of the bare hand shall be considered illegal equipment. A misconduct penalty shall be imposed on any player wearing such a glove in play.

(c) Except for Adults, no player or goalkeeper shall be permitted on the ice while wearing jewelry unless it is completely covered by equipment or taped to the body.

Rule 306 Puck

(a) The puck shall be made of vulcanized rubber or other approved material, one inch thick and three inches in diameter and shall weigh between five and one-half ounces and six ounces and be black in color.

(b) For the 8-or-under (Youth) and for the 8-or-under (Girls) and below age classifications, it is required that the puck weigh between four ounces and four and one-half ounces and be blue in color. It is strongly recommended that the 10-or-under (Youth) and the 10-or-under (Girls) age classifications use the lightweight blue puck.

Rule 307 Equipment Measurement

(a) A request for measurement of any equipment covered by this section shall be limited to one request by each team during the course of any stoppage of play.

(b) The Referee may, at his own discretion, measure any equipment, other than a stick, used for the first time in the game.

(c) The Referee shall assess a bench minor penalty against a
     team that requests any measurement (excluding mouthpiece)
     if the measurement verifies that the equipment is legal.

Rule 308 Electronic Devices

a) The use of one or two-way radios, lights or other electronic
    devices as a means for Team Officials or spectators to
    communicate with players or goalkeepers shall be prohibited.
    For violation, the device will be removed and the team
    assessed a bench minor penalty.

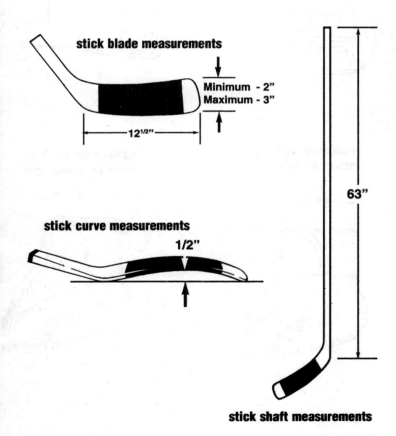

stick blade measurements

Minimum - 2"
Maximum - 3"

12¹/₂"

stick curve measurements

1/2"

63"

stick shaft measurements

Equipment

goalkeeper leg pad measurements

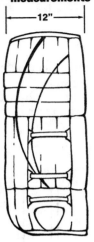

12"

goalkeeper blocker measurements

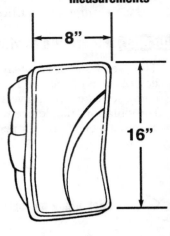

8"

16"

goalkeeper cuff measurements

8$^{1/2}$"

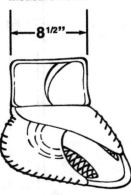

goalkeeper catching glove circumference

48" Maximum

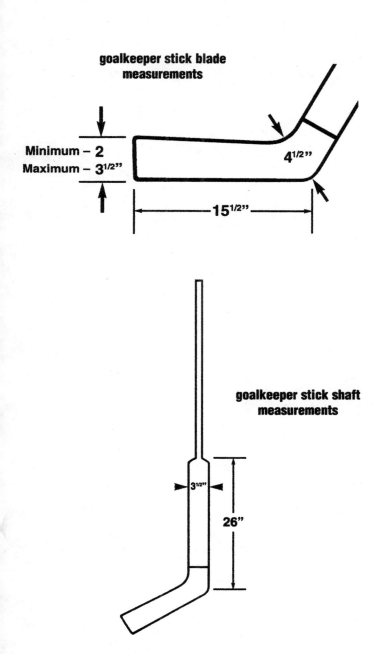

goalkeeper stick blade
measurements

Minimum – 2
Maximum – 3¹/²"

4¹/²"

15¹/²"

goalkeeper stick shaft
measurements

3¹/²"

26"

Equipment

SECTION FOUR
PENALTIES

Rule 401 Penalties

(a) Penalties shall be actual playing time and shall be divided into the following classes:

(1) Minor/Bench Minor Penalties

(2) Major Penalties

(3) Misconduct Penalties

(4) Match Penalties

(5) Penalty Shot

Where coincident penalties are imposed on players of both teams, the penalized players of the visiting team shall take their positions on the penalty bench first in the place designated for visiting players or, where there is no special designation, then on the bench farthest from the gate.

(Note) When play is not actually in progress and an offense is committed by any player or Team Official, the same penalty shall apply as though play were actually in progress.

Rule 402 Minor Penalties

(a) For a "MINOR PENALTY," any player, other than a goalkeeper, shall be ruled off the ice for two minutes during which time no substitute shall be permitted.

(b) For a "BENCH MINOR" penalty one player of the team against which the penalty is imposed shall be ruled off the ice for a period of two minutes, during which time no substitute shall be permitted. Any nonpenalized player of the team who was on the ice at the time of the infraction, except the goalkeeper, may be designated to serve the penalty by the Manager or Coach through the playing Captain, and such player shall take his place on the penalty bench promptly.

(c) If the opposing team scores a goal while a team is shorthanded (below the numerical strength of its opponent on the ice at the time of the goal) by one or more minor penalties, one of such penalties shall automatically terminate. The penalty that terminates automatically is the first minor or bench minor penalty (noncoincident) then being served by the "shorthanded" team. Thus, if an equal number of players from each team is each serving a penalty(s) (minor, bench minor, major or match only), neither team is "shorthanded."

This rule shall not apply when a goal is scored on a penalty shot or an awarded goal.

(d) When the minor penalties of two players of the same team terminate at the same time the Captain of that team shall designate to the Referee which of such players will return to the ice first and the Referee will instruct the Penalty Timekeeper accordingly.

(e) When a player receives a major penalty and a minor penalty at the same time the major penalty shall be served first by the penalized player except under Rule 403(c) in which case the minor penalty will be recorded and served first.

(Note) This applies to the case where BOTH penalties are imposed on the SAME player. See also Note to Rule 408 (Delayed Penalties).

(f) When coincident minor penalties are imposed against players of both teams, the penalized players shall take their place on the penalty bench and such penalized players shall not leave the penalty bench until the first stoppage of play following the expiration of their respective penalties. Immediate substitutions shall be made for an equal number of minor penalties or coincident minor penalties of equal duration to each team so penalized and the penalties of the players for whom substitutions have been made shall not be taken into account for the purpose of a delayed penalty under Rule 408 (Delayed Penalties).

Rule 403 Major Penalties

(a) For the first "MAJOR PENALTY" in any one game, the offender, except the goalkeeper, shall be ruled off the ice for five minutes, during which time no substitute shall be permitted.

(b) For the second major penalty in the same game to the same player or goalkeeper, that player shall be assessed a game misconduct penalty in addition to the major penalty. The player or goalkeeper shall be suspended for his team's next two games. This two-game suspension is in addition to any other required suspensions incurred during the same incident. Unless immediate substitution is permitted under the coincident major penalty Rule 403(c), the penalized team shall immediately place a nonpenalized player other than a goalkeeper on the penalty bench and such player may not be changed.

(c) When coincident major penalties or coincident penalties of equal duration including a major penalty are imposed against players of both teams, the penalized players shall all take their place on the penalty bench and such penalized players shall not leave the penalty bench until the first stoppage of play following the expiration of their respective penalties.

Immediate substitutions shall be made for an equal number of major penalties or coincident penalties of equal duration including a major penalty to each team so penalized and the penalties of the players for which substitutions have been made shall not be taken into account for the purpose of a delayed penalty under Rule 408 (Delayed Penalties).

(d) Where it is required to determine which of the penalized players shall be designated to serve the delayed penalty under Rule 408 (Delayed Penalties), the penalized team shall have the right to make such designation not in conflict with Rule 402 (Minor Penalties).

Rule 404　Misconduct Penalties

(a) A "MISCONDUCT" penalty involves the removal of a player, other than a goalkeeper, from the game for a period of 10 minutes, but another player is permitted to immediately replace a player so removed. A player whose misconduct penalty has expired shall remain in the penalty bench until the next stoppage of play.

Unless immediate substitution is permitted under the coincident penalty rules 402(f) and 403(c), when a player receives a minor or a major penalty plus a misconduct or game misconduct penalty at the same time, the penalized team shall immediately place an additional nonpenalized player other than a goalkeeper on the penalty bench and such player may not be changed.

Any violation of this provision shall be treated as illegal substitution under Rule 205 (Change of Players) calling for a bench minor penalty.

(b) A "GAME MISCONDUCT" penalty involves the suspension of a player or Team Official for the balance of the game, but another player is permitted to immediately replace a player removed.

(c) A player or Team Official incurring a game misconduct penalty shall be suspended for his team's next game (the game already appearing on the schedule of that team at the time of the infraction), except that when such penalty is imposed under Rule 403(b) (Second Major in Game) there shall be a minimum two-game suspension.

(Note) In all cases where a game misconduct penalty is assessed, the incident shall be reported to the proper authorities who shall have full power to impose further suspensions.

(d) Any player (Midget age classification and below, including High School and Senior Women) who incurs five penalties in the same game shall be assessed a game misconduct penalty.

Any Adult player who incurs five penalties in the same game shall be immediately ejected from the game with no further suspension.

Any Head Coach whose team (Midget age classification and below, including High School and Senior Women) receives 15 or more penalties during one game shall be suspended for the next one game of that team.

(Note) For all game misconduct penalties regardless of when imposed, a total of 10 minutes shall be charged in the records against an offending player.

(e) If any Team Official is assessed a game misconduct penalty, he may not sit near the bench of his team, nor in any way attempt to direct the play of his team.

Rule 405 Match Penalties

(a) A "MATCH" penalty involves the suspension of a player or Team Official for the balance of the game, and the offender shall be removed from the game immediately. Unless immediate substitution is permitted under the coincident penalty rules 403(c) and 405(b), the penalized team shall immediately place a nonpenalized player other than a goalkeeper on the penalty bench to serve the time portion (five minutes) of the match penalty, as prescribed by the applicable rule, and such player may not be changed. The player shall also serve any additional minor or major penalty assessed to the offending player or Team Official unless immediate substitution is permitted under the coincident penalty rules 402(f) and 403(c).

(Note) For all "MATCH" penalties, regardless of when imposed, or prescribed additional penalties, a total of 10 minutes shall be charged in the records against the offending player or Team Official.

(b)　When coincident match penalties have been imposed or when any combination of coincident major and match penalties have been imposed on a player or players of both teams, Rule 403(c) covering coincident major penalties will be applicable with respect to player substitutions.

(c)　A player or Team Official incurring a match penalty shall be suspended from participating in any USA Hockey games and practices until his case has been dealt with by the proper authorities. A mandatory hearing by the proper authorities shall be held and a decision made relative to any further disciplinary action within 30 days of the incident. If extenuating circumstances prevent the proper authorities from conducting the mandatory hearing, the player or Team Official shall be automatically reinstated after 30 days.

(Note) The Referee is required to report all match penalties and the surrounding circumstances to the proper authorities immediately following the game in which they occur.

(d)　If any Team Official is assessed a match penalty, he may not sit near the players' bench of his team, nor in any way attempt to direct the play of his team.

(e)　Original jurisdiction in any hearing resulting from a match penalty assessed under Rule 601(g.1) or 601(j.1) (Physical Assault of Officials) shall reside with the Affiliate Association.

Rule 406　Penalty Shot

(a)　A "Penalty Shot" shall be taken as follows:

The Referee shall cause to be announced over the public address system the name of the player designated by him or selected by the team entitled to take the shot (as appropriate) and shall then place the puck on the center face-off spot and the player taking the shot will, on the instruction of the Referee, play the puck from there and shall attempt to score on the goalkeeper. Once the player taking the shot has touched the puck, it must be kept in motion towards the opponent's goal line and once it is shot the play shall be considered complete. No goal can be scored on a rebound of any kind and any time the puck crosses the goal line the shot shall be considered complete.

Only a player designated as a goalkeeper, substitute goalkeeper or temporary goalkeeper (see Glossary) may defend against a penalty shot.

(b)   The goalkeeper must remain in his crease until the player taking the penalty shot has touched the puck and in the event of violation of this rule or any foul committed by a goalkeeper the Referee shall allow the shot to be taken and if the shot fails he shall permit the penalty shot to be taken again.

The goalkeeper may attempt to stop the shot in any manner except by throwing his stick or any object, in which case a minor penalty shall be assessed to the goalkeeper, whether or not a goal is scored on the penalty shot.

(Note) See Rule 636 (Throwing Stick).

(c)   In cases where a penalty shot has been awarded under Rule 609(c)-deliberately displacing goalpost or removing helmet/facemask during a breakaway, Rule 621(f)-interference, under Rule 625(g)-for illegal entry into the game, under Rule 636(a)-for throwing a stick and under Rule 639(c)-for fouling from behind, the Referee shall designate the player who has been fouled as the player who shall take the penalty shot.

In cases where a penalty shot has been awarded under Rule 205(c)-deliberate illegal substitution with less than two minutes remaining in regulation time or anytime during overtime, under Rule 609(c)-deliberately displacing goalpost with less than two minutes remaining in regulation time or anytime during overtime, Rule 612(c)-falling on the puck in the crease or Rule 615(d)-picking up the puck from the crease area, the penalty shot shall be taken by a player selected by the Captain of the nonoffending team from the players on the ice at the time the foul was committed. Such selection shall be reported to the Referee and cannot be changed.

If by reason of injury the player designated by the Referee to take the penalty shot is unable to do so within a reasonable time, the shot may be taken by a player selected by the Captain of the nonoffending team from the players on the ice at the time the foul was committed. Such selection shall be reported to the Referee and cannot be changed.

If the offense for which the penalty shot was awarded was such as would normally incur a minor or bench minor penalty, the nonoffending team may, prior to the penalty shot, elect that the minor or bench minor penalty be assessed to the offending player or team in lieu of the penalty shot.

(d) Should the player in respect to whom a penalty shot has been awarded himself commit a foul in connection with the same play or circumstances, either before or after the penalty shot has been awarded, be designated to take the shot, he shall first be permitted to do so before being sent to the penalty bench to serve the penalty, except when such a penalty is for a game misconduct or match penalty, in which case the penalty shot shall be taken by a player selected by the Captain of the nonoffending team from the players on the ice at the time the foul was committed.

If, at the time a penalty shot is awarded, the goalkeeper of the penalized team has been removed from the ice for another player, the goalkeeper shall be permitted to return to the ice before the penalty shot is taken.

(e) While the penalty shot is being taken, players of both sides shall withdraw to the sides of the rink and beyond the center red line.

(f) If, while the penalty shot is being taken, any player of the opposing team shall have by some action interfered with or distracted the player taking the shot and because of such action the shot should have failed, a second attempt shall be permitted and the Referee shall impose a misconduct penalty on the player so interfering or distracting.

Penalties

(g) If a goal is scored from a penalty shot, the puck shall be faced at center ice in the usual way. If a goal is not scored, the puck shall be faced at either of the end face-off spots in the zone in which the penalty shot has been tried.

(h) Whether or not a goal is scored from a penalty shot, if the offense for which the penalty shot was awarded was such as to incur:

(1) a major, match or misconduct penalty, such penalty shall be imposed in addition to the penalty shot.

(2) a minor or bench minor penalty, the offending team shall not be reduced in on-ice strength as a result.

(i) If the foul upon which the penalty shot is based occurs during actual playing time, the penalty shot shall be awarded and taken immediately in the usual manner, notwithstanding any delay occasioned by a slow whistle by the Referee to permit the play to be completed which delay results in the expiration of the regular playing time in any period.

The time required for the taking of a penalty shot shall not be included in the regular playing time or any overtime.

Rule 407 | Goalkeeper Penalties

(a) A goalkeeper shall not be sent to the penalty bench for an offense that incurs a minor, major or misconduct penalty, but instead any of these penalties shall be served by another member of his team who was on the ice when the offense was committed, such player to be designated by the Manager or Coach of the offending team through the Captain and such substitute shall not be changed.

(b) Should a goalkeeper incur a game misconduct penalty, his place will be taken by a member of his own team, or by a substitute or temporary goalkeeper who is available, and such player will be allowed the goalkeeper's full equipment. He shall also be suspended under the appropriate game misconduct rule (404(c)).

(c) Should a goalkeeper incur a match penalty, his place will be taken by a member of his own team, or by a substitute goalkeeper who is available, and such player will be allowed the goalkeeper's equipment. However, any additional penalties as specifically called for by the individual rules covering match penalties will apply, and the offending team shall be penalized accordingly; such additional penalty to be served by another member of the team on the ice at the time the offense was committed, said player to be designated by the Manager or Coach of the offending team through the Captain.

(d)   A minor penalty shall be imposed on a goalkeeper who leaves the immediate vicinity of his crease during an altercation.

(Note) All penalties imposed on a goalkeeper, regardless of who serves the penalty, or any substitution, shall be charged in the records against the goalkeeper.

(e)   If a goalkeeper deliberately participates in the play in any manner when he is beyond the center red line, a minor penalty shall be imposed upon him.

Rule 408   Delayed Penalties

(a)   If a third player of any team shall be penalized while two players of the same team are serving penalties, the penalty time of the third player shall not commence until the penalty time of one of the two players already penalized shall have elapsed. Nevertheless, the third player penalized must at once proceed to the penalty bench and may be replaced by a substitute until such time as the penalty time of the penalized player shall commence.

(b)   When any team shall have three players serving penalties at the same time and because of the delayed penalty rule a substitute for the third offender is on the ice, none of the three penalized players on the penalty bench may return to the ice until play has been stopped. When play has been stopped, the player whose full penalty has expired may return to the play.

Provided, however, that the Penalty Timekeeper shall permit the return to the ice in the order of expiration of their penalties, of a player or players when by reason of the expiration of their penalties the penalized team is entitled to have more than four players on the ice.

Penalties

(c)   In the case of delayed penalties, the Referee shall instruct the Penalty Timekeeper that the penalized players whose penalties have expired shall only be allowed to return to the ice when there is a stoppage of play.

When the penalties of two players of the same team will expire at the same time the Captain of that team will designate to the Referee which of such players will return to the ice first and the Referee will instruct the Penalty Timekeeper accordingly.

When a major and a minor penalty are imposed at the same time on players of the same team, the Penalty Timekeeper shall record the minor as being the first of such penalties.

(Note) This applies to the case where the two penalties are imposed on DIFFERENT players of the same team. See also Rule 402(e) (Note), (Minor Penalties).

Rule 409   Calling of Penalties

(a)   Should an infraction of the rules be committed by a player of the team in possession and control of the puck, the Referee shall immediately stop play and assess the penalty(s) to the offending player(s).

The resulting face-off shall be made at the place where the play was stopped unless the stoppage occurs in the Attacking Zone of the player penalized in which case the face-off shall be made at the nearest face-off spot in the Neutral Zone.

(b)   Should an infraction of the rules be committed by a player of a team NOT in possession and control of the puck the Referee shall signify the calling of a penalty by raising his arm and upon completion of the play by the team in possession will immediately stop play and assess the penalty to the offending player.

(Note 1) There shall be no signal given by the Referee for a misconduct or game misconduct penalty under this section.

(Note 2) "Completion of the play by the team in possession" in this rule means that the puck must have come into the possession and control of an opposing player or goalkeeper, or has been "frozen." This does not mean a rebound off the goalkeeper, the goal or the boards or any accidental contact with the body or equipment of an opposing player.

The resulting face-off shall be made at the place where the play was stopped, unless during the period of a delayed whistle due to a foul by a player of the team NOT in possession, the team in possession ices the puck, shoots the puck from its Defending Zone so that it goes out of bounds or is unplayable then the face-off following the stoppage shall take place in the Neutral Zone near the defending blue line of the team shooting the puck.

If the penalty or penalties to be imposed are minor penalties and a goal is scored on the play by the nonoffending team, the first minor penalty shall not be imposed but all other penalties shall be imposed in the normal manner regardless of whether or not a goal is scored.

(c) If after the Referee has signaled a penalty but before the whistle has been blown the puck shall enter the goal of the nonoffending team as the direct result of the action of a player of that team, the goal shall be allowed and the penalty signaled shall be imposed in the normal manner.

(d) If the Referee signals an additional minor penalty(s) against a team that is already shorthanded (below the numerical strength of its opponent on the ice at the time of the goal) because of one or more minor or bench minor penalties, and a goal is scored by the nonoffending team before the whistle is blown, the goal shall be allowed, the delayed penalty(s) shall be assessed and the first noncoincident minor penalty already being served shall terminate automatically under Rule 402(c) (Minor Penalties).

(e) Should the same offending player commit other fouls on the same play, either before or after the Referee has blown his whistle, the offending player shall serve such penalties consecutively.

(f) All minor and bench minor penalties occurring after a goal has been scored or during the stoppage of play when a penalty shot is being attempted, shall be served in the normal manner under this rule.

Penalties

Rule 410 Supplementary Discipline

(a)   In addition to the suspensions imposed under these rules, the proper disciplinary authority may, at the conclusion of the game, at their discretion, investigate any incident that occurs in connection with any game and may assess additional suspensions for any offense committed before the game, during the course of a game or any aftermath thereof by a player or Team Official, whether or not such offense has been penalized by the Referee.

(b)   Suspensions imposed during a USA Hockey State, District or Regional Play-Off, or during a National Championship, must be served during that same Play-Off or Championship. If the length of suspension carries beyond that Play-Off for an advancing team, the Discipline Committee of the following Play-Off or Championship shall be the sole authority in determining the eligibility of the individual(s).

(c)   In the case of a Match penalty, the proper disciplinary authority (as defined in the Glossary) shall be required to conduct any disciplinary actions in accordance with the provisions of USA Hockey's "Resolutions of Disputes, Arbitration and Suspensions" section of the current USA Hockey Annual Guide.

SECTION FIVE
OFFICIALS

Rule 501 Appointment of Officials

(a) For Regional and National Championships, the District Referee-in-Chief or his duly appointed representative shall appoint the Referees and Linesmen.

Tournament officials shall appoint a Game Timekeeper, a Penalty Timekeeper, an Official Scorer and two Goal Judges.

(b) Referee System-The official method of refereeing USA Hockey games is with a Referee and two Linesmen. However, Districts or Regions are authorized to use two Referees for games under their jurisdiction. When reference is made to Linesmen under Rule 503 (all clauses) the duties of the Linesmen will be carried out by both Referees in the two-official system.

Rule 502 Referee

(a) The "REFEREE" shall have general supervision of the game and shall have full control of all game officials, team officials and players before, during and after the game, including stoppages; and in case of any dispute, his decision shall be final. The Referee may not change the decision, or that of any other official, after the resumption of play following the rendering of the original decision.

On-Ice Officials should enter the ice surface prior to warm-ups and remain on the ice at the conclusion of each period until all players have proceeded to their dressing rooms. Penalties may also be assessed during the warm-up period.

(b) All On-Ice Officials shall wear black trousers, official sweaters and a black hockey helmet, with helmet strap fastened. It is strongly recommended that all On-Ice Officials wear a half-shield visor properly attached to their helmets. All On-Ice Officials shall wear the current USA Hockey officiating crest on the left chest of the sweater during all games. Any other crest that is worn must be located on either arm of the sweater. They shall be equipped with whistles and metal tape measures with minimum length of six feet. The wearing of name-plates shall be regulated by each League.

Officials

(c)   The Referee shall order the teams on the ice at the appointed time for the beginning of a game and at the commencement of each period. If for any reason there are more than 15 minutes delay in the commencement of the game or any undue delay in resuming play after the 15 minute intervals between periods, the Referee shall state in his report to the proper authorities the cause of the delay and the team or teams that were at fault.

(d)   When he becomes aware of any lack of conformity to the regulations on equipment, it shall be his duty to see that the required equipment is in use.

(e)   The Referee shall, before starting a game, see that the appointed Game Timekeeper, Penalty Timekeeper, Official Scorer and Goal Judges are in their respective places, and satisfy himself that the timing and signaling equipment is in order.

(f)   It shall be his duty to impose such penalties as are prescribed by the rules for infractions thereof, and he shall give the final decision in matters of disputed goals. The Referee may consult with the Linesmen or Goal Judges before making his decision.

(g)   The Referee shall announce to the Official Scorer or Penalty Timekeeper all goals and assists legally scored as well as penalties, and for what infractions such penalties are imposed.

The Referee shall cause to be announced over the public address system the reason for not allowing a goal every time the goal signal light is turned on in the course of play. This shall be done at the first stoppage of play regardless of any signal given by the Referee when the goal signal light was put on in error.

The Referee shall report to the Official Scorer the name or number of the goal scorer and any players entitled to assists.

(Note) The name of the scorer and any player entitled to an assist will be announced on the public address system. In the event that the Referee disallows a goal for any violation of the rules, he shall report the reason for disallowance to the Official Scorer who shall announce the Referee's decision over the public address system.

The infraction of the rules for which each penalty has been imposed will be announced correctly, as reported by the Referee, over the public address system. Where players of both teams are penalized on the same play, the penalty to the visiting player will be announced first.

(h) The Referee shall see to it that players of opposing teams are separated on the penalty bench to prevent feuding.

(i) If, through misadventure or sickness, the Referee and/or Linesmen appointed are prevented from appearing, the Managers or Coaches of the two teams shall agree on a Referee and Linesmen. If they are unable to agree, they shall appoint a player from each team who shall act as Referee and Linesman; the player of the home team acting as Referee, and the player of the visiting team as Linesman.

(j) If the regularly appointed officials appear during the progress of the game, they shall at once replace the temporary officials.

(k) Should an appointed Linesman be unable to act at the last minute or through sickness or accident be unable to finish the game, the Referee shall have the power to appoint another, in his stead, if he deems it necessary, or if required to do so by the Manager or Coach of either of the competing teams.

(l) If for any reason one Official is unable to continue to officiate (three-official system), the game shall be officiated with one Referee/one Linesman or with two Referees as mandated by the local governing body.

(m) The Referee shall check team rosters and all players in uniform before signing reports of the game.

Rule 503 Linesman

(a) The duties of the "LINESMAN" are to determine any infractions of the rules concerning off-side play at the blue lines, at the center line, or any violation of the "Icing the Puck" rule.

He shall stop play when the puck goes outside the playing area, when it is interfered with by any ineligible person, when it is struck above the height of the shoulder, when it is

Officials

passed to a teammate with the hand and when the goal post has been displaced from its normal position. When he is in the near vicinity of the goal, he shall stop play when he observes the puck enter the goal. He shall stop play for off-sides occurring at the face-off circles. He shall stop play when there has been a premature substitution for a goalkeeper under Rule 205(a) (Change of Players), for injured players under Rule 206(e), and interference by spectators under Rule 622(a).

(b)   He shall conduct the face-off at all times, except at the start of the game, at the beginning of each period and after a goal has been scored.

The Referee may call upon a Linesman to conduct a face-off at any time.

(c)   He shall, when requested to do so by the Referee, give his version of any incident that may have taken place during the playing of the game.

(d)   He shall not stop play to report any penalty except any violation of Rule 205(a) and (c), Change of Players (too many players on the ice) and any violation of Rules 601(c.2) and 601(h.3) (articles thrown on the ice from vicinity of players' or penalty bench), and he shall report such violation to the Referee who shall impose a bench minor penalty against the offending team.

He shall report immediately to the Referee his version of the circumstances with respect to Rule 609(c) (delaying the game by deliberately displacing the goal post from its normal position).

He shall report to the Referee at the next stoppage of play his version of any infraction of the rules that he believes constitutes a bench minor, major, match, misconduct, game misconduct or penalty shot under these rules, or any Injury Potential Penalty (See Glossary) that occurs behind the play and is not observed by the Referee. The Referee, at his discretion, may assess a penalty for such infractions.

(e)   Should an Official accidentally leave the ice or receive an injury that incapacitates him from discharging his duties while play is in progress, the game shall be immediately stopped by an On-Ice Official.

Rule 504 | Goal Judge

(a) There shall be one "GOAL JUDGE" at each goal. They shall not be members of either team engaged in a game, nor shall they be replaced during its progress unless after the commencement of the game it becomes apparent that either Goal Judge, on account of partisanship or any other cause, is guilty of giving unjust decisions, in which case the Referee may appoint a replacement.

(b) Goal Judges shall be stationed behind the goals during the progress of play, in properly screened cages, so that there can be no interference with their activities; and they shall not change goals during the game.

(c) In the event of a goal being claimed, the Goal Judge of that goal shall decide whether or not the puck has passed between the goal posts, under the crossbar and entirely over the goal line. His decision is simply "goal" or "no goal."

Rule 505 | Penalty Timekeeper

(a) The "PENALTY TIMEKEEPER" shall keep, on the official forms provided, a correct record of all penalties imposed by the On-Ice Officials including the names of the players penalized, the infractions penalized, the duration of each penalty and the time at which each penalty was imposed. He shall report to the Referee any player or Team Official who is in violation of Rule 404(d) (Game Misconduct). He shall report in the Penalty Record each penalty shot awarded, the name of the player taking the shot and the result of the shot.

(b) The Penalty Timekeeper shall check and ensure that the time served by all penalized players is correct. He shall be responsible for the correct posting of all penalties on the scoreboard at all times and shall promptly call to the attention of the Referee any discrepancy between the time recorded on the clock and the official correct time and he shall be responsible for making any adjustments ordered by the Referee.

He shall, upon request, give a penalized player correct information as to the unexpired time of his penalty.

Officials

(Note 1) The infraction of the rules for which each penalty has been imposed will be announced twice over the public address system as reported by the Referee. Where players of both teams are penalized on the same play, the penalty to the visiting player will be announced first.

(Note 2) Misconduct penalties and coincident minor or major penalties should not be recorded on the timing device, but such penalized players should be alerted and released at the first stoppage of play following the expiration of their penalties.

Rule 506 Official Scorer

(a) Before the start of the game, the "OFFICIAL SCORER" shall obtain from the Manager or Coach of both teams a list of all eligible players of each team, which information shall be made known to the opposing team Manager or Coach before the start of play, either personally or through the Referee.

The Official Scorer shall secure the names of the Captain and Designated Alternate(s) from the Manager or Coach and will so indicate by placing the letter "C" or "A" opposite their names on the scoresheet. For Youth and Girls/Women games (19-or-younger), prior to the start of the game the Official Scorer shall obtain on the scoresheet the signatures of all coaches of each team, one of whom shall be designated as Head Coach, along with the CEP card number, CEP level and the year the CEP level was attained for each coach. This information shall be presented to the Referee for his signature at the completion of the game.

(b) The Official Scorer shall keep a record of the goals scored, the scorers and players to whom assists have been credited, and shall indicate those players on the lists who have actually taken part in the game. He shall also record the time of entry into the game of any substitute or temporary goalkeeper. He shall record on the Official Scoresheet a notation where a goal is scored when the goalkeeper has been removed from the ice.

(c) The awards of points for goals and assists shall be announced over the public address system and all changes in such awards shall also be announced in the same manner.

No requests for changes in any award of points shall be considered unless they are made at or before the conclusion of actual play in the game by the team Captain.

(d) The Official Scorer shall also prepare the Official Scoresheet for signature by the Referee and forward it to the proper authorities.

Rule 507 Game Timekeeper

(a) The "GAME TIMEKEEPER" shall signal the Referee and the competing teams for the start of the game and each succeeding period, and the Referee shall start the play promptly in accordance with Rule 637 (Time of Match). To assist in assuring the prompt return to the ice of the teams and On-Ice Officials, the Game Timekeeper shall give a preliminary warning three minutes prior to the resumption of play in each period.

(b) If the rink is not equipped with an automatic gong, bell or siren, or if such device fails to function, the Game Timekeeper shall signal the end of each period by ringing a gong or bell or by blowing a whistle.

(c) He shall cause to be announced on the public address system at the appropriate time in each period that there is one minute remaining to be played in the period.

(d) The Game Timekeeper shall not sound the horn or buzzer during play to notify the Referee of a malfunction of the clock or any other equipment. He shall note the time and, when play is stopped, notify the Referee of the problem. In the event of any dispute regarding time, the matter shall be referred to the Referee for adjustment and his decision shall be final.

Rule 508 Proper Authorities

(a) The term "proper authorities" or "proper disciplinary authority" as applied under these rules is defined as the governing body of the team or teams involved, as determined by the Affiliate.

Officials

SECTION SIX
PLAYING RULES

Rule 601 Abuse of Officials and Other Misconduct

(Note) In the enforcement of this rule the Referee has, in many instances, the option of imposing a "bench minor penalty," "minor penalty" or a "misconduct penalty." In principle the Referee is directed to impose a "bench minor penalty" in respect to the violations that occur on or in the immediate vicinity of the players' bench but off the playing surface, and in all cases affecting nonplaying personnel or players. A "minor penalty" or "misconduct penalty" should be imposed for violations that occur on the playing surface or in the penalty bench area and where the penalized player is readily identifiable.

An infraction covered under Rules 601(a) through (c) that occurs after the game shall be initially penalized under Rule 601(d).

(a) Any player who challenges or disputes the rulings of any Official or endeavors to incite an opponent (including taunting) or create a disturbance during the game shall be assessed a minor penalty for unsportsmanlike conduct. If the player persists in such challenge or dispute, he shall be assessed a misconduct penalty, and any further dispute by the same player will result in a game misconduct penalty being assessed.

(b) Any player who shoots the puck after the whistle has been blown shall be assessed a minor penalty for unsportsmanlike conduct if, in the opinion of the Referee, the player had sufficient time after the whistle to refrain from taking such shot.

(c) If any player is guilty of any one of the following, his team shall be assessed a bench minor penalty:

(1) In the vicinity of the players' bench, using obscene, profane or abusive language to any person or using the name of any Official coupled with any vociferous remarks.

(2) In the vicinity of the players' bench or penalty bench, throwing anything into the playing area during the progress of the game or during a stoppage of play.

(d) If any player is guilty of any one of the following, he shall be assessed a misconduct penalty:

Playing Rules

---

(1) Using obscene, profane or abusive language to any person on the ice or anywhere in the rink before, during or after the game.

(2) During a stoppage, intentionally knocking, throwing or shooting the puck out of reach of an Official who is retrieving it.

(3) Deliberately throwing the stick, or any other equipment, out of the playing area at any time.

(4) After being penalized, not proceeding directly and immediately to the penalty bench and taking his place on the penalty bench, or to the dressing room, when so ordered by the Referee (gloves, stick, etc., shall be delivered to him at the penalty bench or dressing room by a teammate).

(5) Entering or remaining in the Referee's crease while the Referee is reporting to or consulting with any Game Official including Linesmen, Timekeeper, Penalty Timekeeper, Official Scorer or Announcer except for the purpose of taking his place on the penalty bench.

(6) Interfering in any nonphysical manner with any Game Official including Referee, Linesman, Timekeepers or Goal Judges in the performance of their duties.

(e) If any player is guilty of any one of the following, he shall be assessed a misconduct or game misconduct penalty:

(1) Touching or holding the Referee, Linesman or any other Game Official with his hand or stick.

(2) Continuing or attempting to continue a fight or altercation after he has been ordered by the Referee to stop, or resisting the Linesman in the discharge of his duties.

(3) Intentionally banging the boards, protective glass, dasher boards or goal with a stick or any other instrument at any time. (If the offense is committed in protest of an official's decision, a minor penalty for unsportsmanlike conduct plus a misconduct or game misconduct shall be assessed the offending player.)

(f) If any player is guilty of any one of the following, he shall be assessed a game misconduct penalty:

(1) Persisting in any course of conduct for which he has previously been assessed a misconduct penalty.

(2) Using obscene gestures or racial/ethnic slurs on the ice or anywhere in the rink before, during or after the game.

(g) If any player is guilty of any of the following, he shall be assessed a match penalty:

(1) Deliberately inflicting physical harm to a Game Official in any manner or attempting to do so.

(Note) Any game official assessing a match penalty under Rule 601(g)1 shall file with their USA Hockey District Referee-in-Chief a written game report within 48 hours of the incident.

(2) Deliberately injuring an opposing Team Official in any manner or attempting to do so.

(3) Behaving in any manner that is critically detrimental to the conducting of the game, including spitting at an opponent, spectator, game or team official, or verbally threatening a Game Official with physical harm.

(h) If any Team Official is guilty of any one of the following, his team shall be assessed a bench minor penalty:

(1) Banging the boards with a stick or other instrument at any time.

(2) Using obscene, profane or abusive language or abusive gestures (including taunting) to any person or using the name of any Official coupled with any vociferous remarks.

(3) Throwing anything into the playing area from the vicinity of the players' bench during the game or during a stoppage of play.

(4) Using threatening or abusive language or gestures or similar actions designed to incite an opponent into incurring a penalty.

Playing Rules

    (5) Interfering in any nonphysical manner with any Game Official including the Referee, Linesman, Timekeepers or Goal Judges in the performance of their duties.

(i)   If any Team Official is guilty of any of the following, he shall be assessed a game misconduct penalty:

    (1) Using obscene gestures or racial/ethnic slurs on the ice or anywhere in the rink before, during or after the game.

    (2) Persisting in any course of conduct for which he has previously been assessed a bench minor penalty.

    (3) Interfering in any physical manner with any Game Official, including the Referee, Linesman, Timekeepers or Goal Judges in the performance of their duties.

(j)   If any Team Official is guilty of any one of the following, he shall be assessed a match penalty:

    (1) Deliberately inflicting physical harm to a game official in any manner or attempting to do so.

    (Note) Any game official assessing a match penalty under Rule 601(j)1 shall file with their USA Hockey District Referee-in-Chief a written game report within 48 hours of the incident.

    (2) Deliberately injuring a player or Team Official in any manner or attempting to do so.

    (3) Behaving in any manner that is critically detrimental to the conducting of the game, including spitting at an opponent, spectator, game or team official, or verbally threatening a Game Official, opposing Team Official or opposing player with physical harm.

Rule 602   Adjustment to Clothing and Equipment

(a)   Play shall not be stopped, nor the game delayed by reason of adjustment to clothing, equipment, skates or sticks. For an infringement of this rule, a minor penalty shall be assessed.

(b)   The onus of maintaining clothing and equipment in proper condition shall be upon the player. If adjustments are required, the player shall retire from the ice and play shall continue uninterruptedly with a substitute.

(c) No delay shall be permitted for the repair or adjustment of goalkeeper's equipment. If adjustments are required the goalkeeper will retire from the ice and his place will be taken by the substitute or temporary goalkeeper (See Glossary) immediately and no warm-up will be permitted unless the team uses its time-out. For an infraction of this rule by a goalkeeper, a minor penalty shall be imposed.

Rule 603 Attempt to Injure/Deliberate Injury of Opponents (Head Butting)

(a) A match penalty shall be imposed on any player who deliberately injures or attempts to injure an opponent and the circumstances shall be reported to the proper authorities for further action. A substitute for the penalized player shall be permitted at the end of the fifth minute.

(b) A match penalty shall be imposed on any player or Team Official who deliberately injures or attempts to injure a Team Official or Game Official in any manner and the circumstances shall be reported to the proper authorities for further action.

(c) Any player wearing tape or any other material on his hands who cuts or injures an opponent during an altercation shall receive a match penalty under this rule.

(d) A major plus a game misconduct penalty shall be imposed on any player who "head-butts" in such a manner as to in any way foul an opponent.

(Note) "Head-butting" may also be treated as an Attempt to Injure or Deliberate Injury of an Opponent under Rule 603.

Rule 604 Board-Checking

(a) A minor or a major penalty, at the discretion of the Referee based upon the degree of violence of the impact with the boards, shall be imposed on any player who body-checks, cross-checks, elbows, charges or trips an opponent in such a manner that causes the opponent to be thrown violently into the boards.

Playing Rules

(Note) Any unnecessary contact with a player playing the puck on an obvious "icing" or "off-side" play that results in that player being knocked into the boards is "boarding" and must be penalized as such. In other instances where there is no contact with the boards it should be treated as "charging."

"Rolling" an opponent (if he is the puck carrier) along the boards where he is endeavoring to go through too small an opening is not boarding. However, if the opponent is not the puck carrier, then such action should be penalized as boarding, charging, interference or if the arms or sticks are employed it should be called holding or hooking.

(b)   When a player injures an opponent as the result of "boarding," the Referee shall have no alternative but to impose a major plus a game misconduct penalty on the offending player.

Rule 605   Broken Stick

(a)   A player without a stick may participate in the game. A player or goalkeeper whose stick is broken may participate in the game provided he drops the stick. A minor penalty shall be imposed for an infraction of this rule.

(Note) A broken stick is one that, in the opinion of the Referee, is unfit for normal play.

(b)   A replacement for a stick that is either broken or no longer in possession of a player or goalkeeper may only be obtained from the players' bench or a teammate on the ice. For a violation of this rule a bench minor penalty shall be assessed to the team of the player receiving the replacement stick provided that no penalty is assessed under Rule 601(c.2) or (h.3) for this infraction.

The team, a member of which throws a replacement stick into the playing area, must be penalized under Rule 601(c.2) or (h.3), Throwing Articles into the Playing Area. A player receiving a stick so thrown shall not be penalized.

(Note) The intent of this rule is to provide for the assessment of one penalty for any one illegal stick replacement.

(c)   A goalkeeper whose stick is broken may not go to the players' bench for a replacement during a stoppage of play, but must receive his stick from a teammate.

For an infraction of this rule a minor penalty shall be imposed on the goalkeeper.

Rule 606 Charging

(a)   A minor or a major penalty shall be imposed on a player who runs or jumps into or charges an opponent.

(Note) If more than two steps or strides are taken, it shall be considered "charging."

When a player injures an opponent as the result of "Charging" the Referee shall have no alternative but to impose a major plus a game misconduct penalty on the offending player.

(b)   A minor or a major penalty shall be imposed on a player who body checks or charges a goalkeeper while the goalkeeper is within his goal crease or privileged area.

A goalkeeper is NOT "fair game" just because he is outside his privileged area. A penalty for interference or charging should be called in every case where an opposing player makes unnecessary contact with a goalkeeper.

Likewise, Referees should be alert to penalize goalkeepers for tripping, slashing or spearing in the vicinity of the goal.

Rule 607 Checking from Behind

(a)   A minor plus a misconduct penalty, or a major plus a game misconduct penalty, shall be imposed on any player who body checks or pushes an opponent from behind.

When a player injures an opponent as the result of "Checking from Behind" the Referee shall have no alternative but to impose a major plus a game misconduct penalty on the offending player.

(Note) Checking from behind may also be treated as Attempt to Injure or Deliberate Injury of an Opponent under Rule 603.

(b)   A major plus a game misconduct penalty shall be imposed on any player who body checks or pushes an opponent from behind head first into the side boards, end boards or goal frame.

Playing Rules

Rule 608 Cross-Checking or Butt-Ending

(a)   A minor or a major penalty shall be imposed on a player who "cross-checks" an opponent.

(Note) "Cross-check" shall mean a check delivered with both hands on the stick and no part of the stick on the ice.

(b)   A major plus a game misconduct penalty shall be imposed on any player who injures an opponent by "cross-checking."

(c)   A major plus a game misconduct penalty shall be imposed on any player who "butt-ends" or attempts to "butt-end" an opponent.

(Note 1) Attempt to "butt-end" shall include all cases where a "butt-end" gesture is made regardless of whether body contact is made or not.

(Note 2) "Butt-ending" may also be treated as an Attempt to Injure or Deliberate Injury of an Opponent under Rule 603.

Rule 609 Delaying the Game

(a)   A minor penalty shall be imposed on any player or goalkeeper who delays the game by deliberately shooting or batting the puck with his stick outside the playing area.

(Note) This penalty shall apply also when a player or goalkeeper deliberately bats or shoots the puck with his stick outside the playing area after a stoppage of play.

(b)   A minor penalty shall be imposed on a goalkeeper who shoots the puck directly (nondeflected) outside of the playing area, except that no penalty shall apply if the puck inadvertently leaves the playing area in a location that is not protected by glass or screen.

(c)   A minor penalty shall be imposed on any player (including a goalkeeper) who delays the game by deliberately displacing a goal post from its normal position. The Referee or Linesmen shall stop play immediately when a goal post has been displaced.
      If the defending team has deliberately displaced the goal post, thereby depriving the attacking team of an immediate and reasonable scoring opportunity, or if, during the course of

a break-away, the goalkeeper (all classifications) or player (excluding Adults) deliberately removes his helmet/facemask, a penalty shot/optional minor penalty shall be awarded to the nonoffending team, which shot shall be taken by the player last in possession of the puck.

If a player of the defending team deliberately displaces the goal and, in the opinion of the Referee, the puck would have entered the goal had it not been displaced, or if the defending team deliberately displaces the goal when the goalkeeper is off the ice, thereby preventing an obvious and imminent goal, a goal shall be awarded in lieu of a penalty shot.

(Note) A player with a "break-away" is defined as a player in control of the puck with no opposition between the player and the opposing goal and with a reasonable scoring opportunity.

If a minor penalty for deliberately displacing a goal, or for the goalkeeper (all classifications) or player (excluding Adults) deliberately removing his helmet/facemask during play, is assessed with less than two minutes remaining in regulation time, or at any time during overtime, a penalty shot/optional minor shall be assessed against the offending team in lieu of the minor penalty.

d) A bench minor penalty shall be imposed upon any team that, after warning by the Referee to its Captain to place the correct number of players on the ice and commence play, fails to comply with the Referee's direction and thereby causes any delay by making additional substitutions, by persisting in having its players off-side, including failure to line up properly for a face-off under Rule 611(a), or in any other manner.

e) A minor penalty shall be imposed on a player or goalkeeper who deliberately holds the puck against the boards, goal or ice with his stick, skate, foot or any other part of his body for the purpose of delaying the game (see Rule 612(b), Falling on the Puck).

f) A minor penalty shall be imposed on a goalkeeper who has an opportunity to play the puck with his stick prior to being pressured by an attacking player, but instead intentionally causes a stoppage of play.

Playing Rules

(g)   A minor penalty for delaying the game shall be assessed to a player who, after a warning by the Referee, fails to maintain a proper position during the conducting of a face-off.

Rule 610 Elbowing or Kneeing

(a)   A minor or a major penalty shall be imposed on any player who uses his elbow or knee in such a manner as to in any way foul an opponent.

(b)   A major plus a game misconduct penalty shall be imposed on any player who injures an opponent as the result of a foul committed by elbowing or kneeing.

Rule 611 Face-Offs

(a)   The puck shall be "faced-off" by the Referee or the Linesman dropping the puck on the ice between the sticks of the players "facing-off." Players facing-off will stand squarely facing their opponents' end of the rink approximately one stick length apart with the blade of their sticks touching the ice. The attacking team player shall be the first player to place his stick on the ice. For face-offs along the center red line, the visiting team player shall place his stick on the ice first.

When the face-off takes place at any of the end face-off spots, the players taking part shall be stationary and stand squarely facing their opponents' end of the rink and clear of the ice markings. The sticks of both players facing-off shall have the blade on the ice in contact with the nearest white area of the face-off spot and clear of the red center area of the spot.

No other player shall be allowed to enter the face-off circle or come within 15 feet of the players facing-off the puck, and players other than the player facing off must stand on-side on all face-offs.

If a player, other than the player facing off, fails to maintain his proper position, the center of his team shall be ejected from the face-off.

At the conclusion of the line change procedure, the Official conducting the face-off shall blow his whistle. This will signal each team that they have no more than five seconds to line up for the ensuing face-off. Prior to the conclusion of five seconds, the Official shall conduct a proper face-off. If any player other than the players facing off fails to maintain a proper position, the center of that team shall be ejected from the face-off.

A second violation of any of the provisions of subsection (a) hereof by the same team during the same face-off shall be penalized with a minor penalty to the player who commits the second violation of the rule.

If, after a warning by the Referee or Linesman, either of the players fails to take his proper position for the face-off within five seconds, the Official shall be entitled to face-off the puck notwithstanding such default.

In the conduct of any face-off anywhere on the playing surface, no player facing-off shall make any physical contact with his opponent's body by means of his own body or by his stick except in the course of playing the puck after the face-off has been completed.

For violation of this rule the Referee shall impose a minor penalty or penalties on the player(s) whose action(s) caused the physical contact.

(Note) "Conduct of any face-off" commences when the On-Ice Official designates the place of the face-off and he takes up his position to drop the puck.

If a player facing-off fails to take his proper position immediately when directed by the Official, the Official may order him replaced for that face-off by any teammate then on the ice.

No substitution of players shall be permitted until the face-off has been completed and play has been resumed except when any penalty is imposed.

When an infringement of a rule has been committed or a stoppage of play has been caused by any player of the attacking team in the Attacking Zone the ensuing face-off shall be made in the Neutral Zone on the nearest face-off spot.

Playing Rules

(Note) This includes a stoppage of play caused by a player o the attacking team shooting the puck onto the back of the defending team's goal without any intervening action by th defending team.

(g) When an infringement of a rule resulting in a stoppage has been committed by players from both teams in one play, or when the game is stopped for any reason not specifically covered in these official rules, the puck must be faced off at the nearest point along the imaginary lines on each side connecting the end zone face-off spots to where the puck wa last played.

When an infringement of a rule causes a stoppage of play and the offending team gains a territorial advantage, the ensuing face-off shall be conducted where the stoppage of play occurred.

(h) When a stoppage occurs between the end face-off spots and near end of the rink, the puck shall be faced-off at the end face-off spot on the side where the stoppage occurs, unless otherwise expressly provided by these rules.

(i) When a goal is legally scored the ensuing face-off shall be conducted at center ice. When a goal is illegally scored as a result of a puck being deflected directly from an Official anywhere in the Defending Zone, the resulting face-off shal be made at the end face-off spot in the Defending Zone.

(j) Playing time will commence from the instant the puck is faced-off and will stop when the whistle is blown.

(k) When a stoppage of play in an end zone takes place and is followed by a gathering of players, no attacking player shall enter the end zone further than the outer edge of the face-o circles nearest the blue line (this includes players on the ice at the time of the stoppage of play or players involved in a line change).

For a violation of this rule the ensuing face-off shall take place at the nearest Neutral Zone face-off spot.

Rule 612 Falling on Puck

A minor penalty shall be imposed on a player other than the goalkeeper who deliberately falls on or gathers the puck into his body.

(Note) Any player who drops to his knees to block a shot should not be penalized if the puck is shot under him or becomes lodged in his clothing or equipment, but any use of the hands to make the puck unplayable should be penalized promptly.

A minor penalty shall be imposed on a goalkeeper who deliberately falls on or gathers the puck into his body, when his body is entirely outside the boundaries of the goal crease and the puck is behind the goal line or when the puck is outside the boundaries of the "goalkeeper's privileged area," or who holds or places the puck against any part of the goal or against the boards, or when having an opportunity to play the puck with his stick prior to being pressured by an attacking player. (See also Rules 609(e) and 609(f), Delaying the Game.)

No defending player, except the goalkeeper, shall be permitted to fall on the puck or hold the puck or gather the puck into the body or hands when the puck is within the goal crease.

For an infringement of this rule, play shall immediately be stopped and a penalty shot/optional minor shall be awarded to the nonoffending team. However, if the goalkeeper has been removed from the ice when the infraction occurs, a goal shall be awarded to the nonoffending team and no penalty shot shall be awarded, if the action of the offending player prevents an obvious and imminent goal.

(Note) This rule shall be interpreted so that a penalty shot/optional minor will be awarded only when the puck is in the crease at the instant the infraction occurs. However, in cases where the puck is outside the crease, Rule 612(a) may still apply and a minor penalty may be imposed, even though no penalty shot is awarded.

Rule 613 | Fisticuffs (Fighting)

(a) A major penalty shall be imposed on any player who engage in fisticuffs. An additional minor penalty shall be imposed (any player who starts or instigates fisticuffs.

(b) A minor penalty shall be imposed on a player who, having been struck, shall retaliate with a blow or attempted blow. However, at the discretion of the Referee a double minor or major penalty may be imposed if such player continues the altercation.

(Note 1) The Referee is provided very wide latitude in the penalties that he may impose under this rule. This is done intentionally to enable him to differentiate between the obvious degrees of responsibility of the participants either for starting the fighting or persisting in continuing the fighting. The discretion provided shall be exercised realistically.

(Note 2) Referees are directed to employ every means provided by these rules to stop "brawling" and should use Rule 601(e.2) "Abuse of Officials and Other Misconduct" f(this purpose.

(c) A major penalty shall be imposed on any player involved in fisticuffs off the playing surface or with another player who is off the playing surface before, during or after the game.

(d) A game misconduct penalty shall be imposed on any player or goalkeeper who is the first to intervene in an altercation then in progress. This penalty is in addition to any other penalty incurred in the same incident.

(e) Any player receiving a major penalty for fisticuffs shall automatically also be assessed a game misconduct penalty.

(f) When an altercation occurs on the ice, at the signal of the Referee, all players (nonparticipant), excluding goalkeepers, must proceed immediately and directly to their respective players' bench. Goalkeepers must remain in the immediate vicinity of their goal crease. See Rule 407(d) (Goalkeeper's Penalties). A minor penalty shall be assessed to any player, excluding goalkeepers, who fails to move to the players' bench when so instructed by the Referee.

A minor penalty shall be imposed on any player, including a goalkeeper, who removes his glove or gloves and/or drops his stick during an altercation and who is not a participant in the original altercation. A game misconduct penalty may be added to the minor penalty if, in the judgment of the Referee, the player is the instigator of a subsequent altercation. This penalty shall be in addition to any other penalty incurred in the same incident.

Rule 614 | Goals and Assists

(Note) It is the responsibility of the Referee to award goals and assists, and his decision in this respect is final. Such awards shall be made or withheld strictly in accordance with the provisions of this rule. Therefore, it is essential that the Referee shall be thoroughly familiar with every aspect of this rule, be alert to observe all actions that could affect the making of an award and, above all, the awards must be made or withheld with absolute impartiality.

In cases of an obvious error in awarding a goal or an assist that has been announced, it should be corrected promptly. Changes shall not be made in the official scoring summary after the Referee has signed the Game Report.

A goal shall be scored when the puck shall have been put between the goal posts by the stick of a player of the attacking team, from in front and below the cross bar, and entirely across the goal line.

A goal shall be scored if the puck is put into the goal in any way by a player of the defending team. The player of the attacking team who last played the puck shall be credited with the goal but no assist shall be awarded.

If an attacking player kicks the puck and the puck goes directly into the goal or is deflected into the goal by any player, including the goalkeeper, a goal shall not be allowed.

If the puck shall have been deflected into the goal from the shot of an attacking player by striking any part of a player of the same team, a goal shall be allowed. The player who deflected the puck shall be credited with the goal. The goal shall not be allowed if the puck has been kicked, thrown or otherwise deliberately directed into the goal by any means other than a stick.

(e)   If a goal is scored as a result of a puck being deflected directly into the goal from an Official, the goal shall not be allowed.

(f)   Should a player legally propel a puck into the goal crease of the opposing team and the puck should become loose and available to another player of the attacking team, a goal scored on the play shall be valid.

(g)   Any goal scored, other than as covered by the official rules, shall not be allowed.

(h)   A "goal" shall be credited in the scoring records to a player who shall have propelled the puck into the opponents' goal. Each "goal" shall count one point in the player's record.

(i)   When a player scores a goal, an "assist" shall be credited to the player or players taking part in the play immediately preceding the goal, but not more than two assists can be given on any goal. Each "assist" so credited shall count one point in the player's record.

(j)   Only one point can be credited to any one player on a goal.

Rule 615 Handling Puck with Hands

(a)   If a player, except a goalkeeper, closes his hand on the puck, play shall be stopped and a face-off shall follow; however, if the puck is dropped to the ice immediately, play shall not be stopped.

If a goalkeeper holds the puck with his hand for more than three seconds, play shall be stopped and a face-off shall follow; however, after an initial warning by the Referee, a goalkeeper who holds the puck unnecessarily shall be assessed a minor penalty for delay of game.

(b)   A goalkeeper shall not drop the puck into his pads or onto the goal net, nor deliberately pile up snow or obstacles at or near his goal that, in the opinion of the Referee, would tend to prevent the scoring of a goal. The penalty for infringement of this rule by the goalkeeper shall be a minor penalty.

(Note 1) The object of this rule is to keep the puck in play continuously and any action taken by the goalkeeper that causes an unnecessary stoppage must be penalized.

(Note 2) The goalkeeper may not leave his stick or part thereof in front of his goal. If he does and if the puck hits the stick, thereby preventing an obvious and imminent goal while the goalkeeper is on the ice, but in the act of leaving the ice, or off the ice, the Referee shall stop play and award a goal to the nonoffending team. See Rule 621(f), Interference.

(c)   If a goalkeeper catches the puck and throws it forward towards his opponent's goal and it is first played by a teammate, play shall be stopped and the ensuing face-off shall be held at the nearest end face-off spot of the offending team. (See also Rule 615(e).)

(d)   A minor penalty shall be imposed on a player except the goalkeeper who, while play is in progress, picks up the puck off the ice with his hand.

    If a defending player, except the goalkeeper, while play is in progress, picks up the puck with his hand from the ice in the goal crease or holds the puck while the puck is in the goal crease, the play shall be stopped immediately and a penalty shot/optional minor shall be awarded to the nonoffending team.

    If a defending player picks up the puck from the goal crease or falls on or covers the puck in the crease thereby preventing an obvious and imminent goal when the goalkeeper has been removed from the ice, a goal shall be awarded to the nonoffending team.

(e)   A player or goalkeeper shall be permitted to stop or "bat" the puck in the air with his hand or push it along the ice with his hand and play shall not be stopped unless he has directed the puck to a teammate in any zone other than his Defending Zone, in which case play shall be stopped and the puck faced-off at the spot where the offense occurred unless otherwise provided by these rules.

(Note) No territorial ice advantage can be gained from a team illegally batting the puck with the hand.

A goal shall not be allowed if the puck was propelled by the hand of an attacking player and entered the goal either directly or after deflecting off any player including the goalkeeper.

Rule 616 Head Contact

(a)   A minor penalty, major penalty or a major plus game misconduct penalty, at the discretion of the Referee, shall be assessed to any player who intentionally or recklessly contacts a player in the head, including with the stick or by an illegal body check.

(b)   A major plus a game misconduct penalty shall be imposed on any player who injures an opponent by head contact (see Glossary).

(Note) Head contact may also be treated as Attempt to Injure or Deliberate Injury of an Opponent under Rule 603.

Rule 617 High Sticks

(a)   The carrying of sticks above the normal height of the shoulder is prohibited. The Referee may assess a minor or a major penalty on any player violating this rule.

(Note) The use of the "slap shot" in the 10-or-under age classification and below is prohibited. This applies to both Youth and Girls. A face-off shall take place at one of the end face-off spots adjacent to the goal of the offending player's team who, in the process of making a forehand shot or pass, raises the blade of his stick above his waist in the backswing of such shot or pass.

(b)   A major plus a game misconduct penalty shall be imposed on any player who injures an opponent by the use of a high stick.

(c)   A goal scored from a stick so carried shall not be allowed, except by a player of the defending team.

(d) Batting the puck above the normal height of the shoulders with the stick is prohibited and when it occurs there shall be a whistle and the ensuing face-off shall take place at one of the end face-off spots adjacent to the goal of the team causing the stoppage unless:

(1) the puck is batted to an opponent and the opponent gains possession and control of the puck, in which case the play shall continue, or

(2) a player of the defending team shall bat the puck into his own goal in which case the goal shall be allowed.

(Note) When a player bats the puck to an opponent under subsection 1, the Referee shall give the "washout" signal immediately. Otherwise he will stop the play.

Rule 618　Holding an Opponent

(a) A minor penalty shall be imposed on a player who holds an opponent with hands or stick or in any other way.

(b) A major plus a game misconduct penalty shall be imposed on a player who grabs or holds the facemask of an opponent with his hand.

Rule 619　Hooking

(a) A minor or major penalty shall be imposed on a player who impedes or seeks to impede the progress of an opponent by "hooking" with his stick.

(b) A major plus game misconduct penalty shall be imposed on any player who injures an opponent by "hooking."

Rule 620　Icing the Puck

(a) For the purpose of this rule, the center line will divide the ice into halves. Should any player of a team, equal or superior in numerical strength to the opposing team, shoot, bat with the hand or stick, kick or deflect the puck from his own half of the ice, beyond the goal line of the opposing team, play shall be stopped and the puck faced off at the end face-off spot of

Playing Rules

the offending team. If the puck shall have entered the goal of the opposing team, after being legally shot, batted with the stick or deflected, the goal shall be allowed.

For the purpose of this rule, the point of last contact with the puck by the team in possession shall be used to determine whether icing has occurred or not.

(Note 1) If, during the period of a delayed whistle due to a foul by a player of the side NOT in possession, the side in possession "ices" the puck then the face-off following the stoppage of play shall take place in the Neutral Zone near the defending blue line of the team "icing" the puck.

(Note 2) When a team is "Shorthanded" as the result of a penalty and the penalty is about to expire, the decision as to whether there has been an "icing" shall be determined at the instant the penalty expires, and if the puck is shot before the penalty expires, icing shall not be called. The action of the penalized player remaining in the penalty bench will not alter the ruling.

(Note 3) For the purpose of interpretation of this rule, "Icing the Puck" is completed the instant the puck completely crosses the goal line. If the puck shall have entered the goal, the icing will not be called and a goal shall be allowed.

(Note 4) When the puck is shot and rebounds from the body or stick of an opponent in his own half of the ice so as to cross the goal line of the player shooting it, "icing" shall not be called.

(Note 5) Notwithstanding the provisions of this section concerning "batting" the puck in respect to the "icing the puck" rule, the provisions of the second paragraph of Rule 615(e) "Handling Puck With Hands," apply and NO goal can be scored by batting the puck with the hand into the opponent's goal, whether intended or not.

(Note 6) If, while the Linesman has signaled a slow whistle under Rule 626(f), "Off-Sides," a defending player shoots or bats the puck beyond the opponent's goal line in such a manner as to constitute "icing the puck," the Linesman's "slow whistle" shall be considered exhausted the instant the puck crosses the blue line and icing shall be called in the usual manner.

(b)　If the puck was so shot by a player of a team below the numerical on-ice strength of the opposing team, play shall continue and the face-off shall not take place.

(c)　If, however, the puck shall go beyond the goal line in the opposite half of the ice directly from either of the players while facing-off, it shall not be considered a violation of this rule.

(d)　If, in the opinion of the Linesman, a player of the opposing team excepting the goalkeeper is able to play the puck before it passes the goal line, but has not done so, icing shall not be called and play shall continue.

(Note) The purpose of this section is to enforce continuous action and the On-Ice Officials should interpret and apply the rule to produce this result.

(e)　If the puck shall touch any part of a player of the opposing team or his skates or his stick before it shall have reached the goal line, or shall have touched the goalkeeper or his skates or his stick at any time before crossing his goal line, it shall not be considered as "icing the puck" and play shall continue.

(f)　If the Linesman shall have erred in calling an "icing the puck" infraction (regardless of whether either team is shorthanded) a last play face-off (nearest end zone face-off spot) shall occur.

Rule 621　Interference

(a)　A minor penalty shall be imposed on a player who interferes with or impedes the progress of an opponent who is not in possession of the puck, or who deliberately knocks a stick out of an opponent's hand or who prevents a player who has dropped his stick or any other piece of equipment from regaining possession of it or who knocks or shoots any abandoned or broken stick or illegal puck or other debris towards an opposing puck carrier in a manner that could cause him to be distracted. (See also Rule 636, Throwing Stick.)

Playing Rules

(Note) The last player to touch the puck, other than a goalkeeper, shall be considered the player in possession. In interpreting this rule the Referee should make sure which of the players is the one creating the interference. Often it is the action and movement of the attacking player that causes the interference since the defending players are entitled to "stand their ground" or "shadow" the attacking player. Players of the side in possession shall not be allowed to "run" deliberate interference for the puck carrier.

(b) A minor penalty shall be imposed on any player on the players' bench or on the penalty bench who by means of his stick or his body interferes with the movements of the puck or of any opponent on the ice during the progress of play.

(c) A minor penalty shall be imposed on a player who, by means of his stick or his body, interferes with or impedes the movements of the goalkeeper by actual physical contact, while he is in his goal crease unless the puck is already in the crease.

(d) When the puck is in the Attacking Zone and not in the goal crease, a player of the attacking team may not stand on the goal crease line or in the goal crease, hold his stick in the goal crease or skate through the goal crease. If the puck should enter the goal while such a condition prevails, a goal shall not be allowed. For violation of this rule, while the attacking team has possession of the puck, play shall be stopped and a face-off held at the nearest Neutral Zone face-off spot.

(Note) This rule shall not apply when the goalkeeper is out of his goal crease.

(e) If a player of the attacking team has been physically interfered with by the action of any defending player so as to cause him to be in the goal crease, and the puck should enter the goal while the player so interfered with is still within the goal crease, the "goal" shall be allowed.

(f) When a player in control of the puck beyond the defending blue line, and having no opponent to pass other than the goalkeeper, is interfered with by a stick or part thereof or any other object thrown or shot by any member of the defending team including any Team Official, a penalty shot/optional minor shall be awarded to the nonoffending team.

(Note) The attention of Referees is directed particularly to three types of offensive interference which should be penalized:

(1)When the defending team secures possession of the puck in its own end and the other players of that team run interference for the puck carrier by forming a protective screen against forecheckers;

(2)When a player facing-off obstructs his opponent after the face-off when the opponent is not in possession of the puck;

(3)When the puck carrier makes a drop pass and follows through so as to make bodily contact with an opposing player.

Defensive interference consists of bodily contact with an opposing player who is not in possession of the puck.

Rule 622 | Interference by Spectators

(a)   In the event of a player being held or interfered with by a spectator, the Referee or Linesman shall blow the whistle and play shall be stopped, unless the team of the player interfered with is in possession of the puck at the time, in which case the play shall be allowed to be completed before blowing the whistle, and the puck shall be faced at the spot where last played at the time of stoppage.

(Note) The Referee shall report to the proper authorities for disciplinary action all cases in which a player becomes involved in an altercation with a spectator.

(b)   Any player who physically interferes with a spectator shall be assessed a game misconduct penalty and the Referee shall report all such infractions to the proper authorities who shall have full power to impose such further penalty as deemed appropriate.

Playing Rules

(c)   In the event that objects are thrown on the ice that interfere with the progress of the game, the Referee shall blow the whistle and stop the play and the puck shall be faced-off at the spot where play is stopped.

Rule 623 Kicking Player

(a)   A major plus a game misconduct penalty shall be imposed on any player or goalkeeper who uses their skate to "push off" an opponent. Any kicking motion by a player or goalkeeper must be penalized under subsection (b) below.

(b)   A Match penalty shall be imposed on any player who kicks or attempts to kick another player. If a player or goalkeeper injures an opponent by kicking, a Match penalty shall be assessed.

Rule 624 Kicking Puck

(a)   Kicking the puck shall be permitted in all zones; however, a goal shall not be allowed if the puck was kicked by an attacking player and entered the goal either directly or after deflecting off any player including the goalkeeper.

Rule 625 Leaving the Players' Bench or Penalty Bench

(a)   No player may leave the players' bench or penalty bench at any time during an altercation or for the purpose of starting an altercation. Substitutions made prior to the altercation shall not be penalized under this rule provided the players so substituting do not enter the altercation.

(b)   For violation of this rule, a major plus a game misconduct penalty shall be imposed on any player who leaves the players' bench or penalty bench during an altercation.

(c)   Except at the end of each period, or on expiration of a penalty, no player may at any time leave the penalty bench.

(d)   A penalized player who leaves the penalty bench before his penalty has expired, whether play is in progress or not, shall incur an additional minor penalty after serving his unexpired penalty.

(e) If a player leaves the penalty bench before his penalty is fully served, the Penalty Timekeeper shall note the time and verbally alert the Referee who will stop play when the offending player's team has or gains possession and control of the puck.

(f) In the case of a player returning to the ice before his time has expired through an error of the Penalty Timekeeper, he is not to serve an additional penalty, but must serve his unexpired time.

(g) If a player of an attacking team in possession of the puck shall be in such a position as to have no opposition between him and the opposing goalkeeper, and while in such a position he shall be interfered with by a player of the opposing team who shall have illegally entered the game, the Referee shall impose a penalty shot/optional minor against the offending player's team.

(h) If a Team Official gets on the ice after the start of a period and before that period is ended without the permission of the Referee, the Referee shall impose a bench minor penalty against the team or a game misconduct penalty on the individual or both and report the incident to the proper authorities.

(i) If a penalized player returns to the ice from the penalty bench before his penalty has expired by his own error or the error of the Penalty Timekeeper, any goal scored by his own team while he is illegally on the ice shall be disallowed, but all penalties imposed on either team shall be served as regular penalties.

(j) If a player shall illegally enter the game from his own players' bench or from the penalty bench, any goal scored by his own team while he is illegally on the ice shall be disallowed, but all penalties imposed against either team shall be served as regular penalties.

(k) **(For Youth and all Girls/Women games)**
On any face-off, if a team starts play with fewer players than entitled to, any subsequently entering player shall not be eligible to play any puck coming from his own Defending Zone until he has returned to his own Defending Zone or

until possession and control of the puck has been gained by another player in the Neutral Zone or in his own Attacking Zone.

For a violation of this rule play shall be stopped and a face-off shall be conducted at the point where the puck was last legally played.

Rule 626 Off-Sides

(a) Players of an attacking team may not precede the puck into the Attacking Zone.

(Note) A player actually propelling and in possession and control of the puck who shall cross the line ahead of the puck shall not be considered "off-side."

(b) For a violation of this Rule, play shall be stopped and a face-off conducted.

If the puck was carried over the blue line at the time of the violation, the face-off shall take place at the nearest Neutral Zone face-off spot to where the puck crossed the line. If the puck was passed or shot over the blue line, the face-off shall take place where the pass or shot originated.

(c) The position of the player's skates and not that of his stick shall be the determining factor in deciding an "off-side" violation. A player is off-side when both skates are completely over the outer edge of the blue line into his Attacking Zone.

(Note 1) A player is "on-side" when "either" of his skates are in contact with the Neutral Zone ice or when the entire player, including both skates, is completely behind the determining edge of the blue line, at the instant the puck completely crosses the outer edge of that line, regardless of the position of his stick.

(Note 2) The position of the player's skates is what determines whether a player is "off-side." However, the question of "off-side" never arises until the puck has completely crossed the line into the Attacking Zone, at which time the decision is to be made.

(d)   If a player legally carries or passes the puck back into his own Defending Zone while a player of the opposing team is in such Defending Zone, the "off-side" shall be waived and play permitted to continue. (No "delayed whistle.")

(e)   If, in the opinion of the Linesman, a player has intentionally caused an off-side play (including a puck shot on goal), the puck shall be faced-off at the nearest end zone face-off spot in the Defending Zone of the offending team.

(Note) An intentional off-side is one which is made for the purpose of deliberately securing an immediate stoppage of play, regardless of the reason, or where an off-side play is made under conditions where there is no possibility of completing a legal play.

(f)   **For Adults (male and female) only** — If an attacking player precedes the puck that is shot, passed or deflected into the Attacking Zone, the Linesman shall signal a delayed off-side. The off-side violation will be nullified if all attacking players in the Attacking Zone clear the Attacking Zone by making skate contact with the blue line. The Attacking Zone must be completely clear of attacking players before a delayed off-side can be nullified with the puck still in the Attacking Zone.

During the delayed off-side, the Linesman shall stop play for the off-side violation if ANY attacking player touches the puck or attempts to gain possession of a loose puck while the puck is still in the Attacking Zone or forces the defending puck carrier further back in the Attacking Zone.

(g)   If the Linesman shall have erred in stopping play for an off-side infraction the ensuing face-off shall take place at the nearest Neutral Zone face-off spot to the blue line where play was stopped in error.

Rule 627   Passes

(a)   **(For Youth, Girls/Women and Adult noncrhecking games)**
The puck may be passed by any player to a player of the same team within any of the three zones into which the ice is divided and may be passed forward by a player in his own Defending Zone to a player of the same team anywhere in the Neutral Zone.

(For Adult male checking games)

The puck may be passed by any player to a player of the same side within any one of the three zones into which the ice is divided, but may not be passed forward from a player in one zone to a player of the same side in another zone, except by a player on the defending team, who may make and take forward passes from their own Defending Zone to the center line without incurring an offside violation. This pass, however, must be completed by a receiving player who is legally onside at the center line, or by a receiving player who is preceded by the puck across the center line, otherwise play shall be stopped and the face-off shall be conducted at the spot from which the pass originated.

(Note 1) The position of the puck (not the player's skates) shall be the determining factor in deciding from which zone the pass was made.

(Note 2) Passes may be completed legally at the center red line in exactly the same manner as passes at the attacking blue line.

(b)   Should the puck, having been passed, contact any part of the body, stick or skates of a player of the same team who is legally onside, the pass shall be considered to have been completed.

(c)   The player last touched by the puck shall be deemed to be in possession.

Rebounds off goalkeeper's pad or other equipment shall not be considered as a change of possession or the completion of the play by the team when applying Rule 409(b) (Calling of Penalties).

(d)   **(For Youth, Girls/Women and Adult nonchecking games)**

If the puck precedes all players of the attacking team into their Attacking Zone, any player is eligible to play the puck except when Rule 620 (Icing the Puck) applies.

(For Adult male checking games)

If a player in the Neutral Zone is preceded into the Attacking Zone by the puck passed from the Neutral Zone he shall be eligible to take possession of the puck anywhere in the Attacking Zone except when the "Icing the Puck" rule applies.

(e)   If a player in the same zone from which a pass is made is preceded by the puck into succeeding zones, he shall be eligible to take possession of the puck in that zone except where the "Icing the Puck" rule applies.

(f)   **(For Adult male checking games)**
        If an attacking player passes the puck backward toward his own goal from the Attacking Zone, an opponent may play the puck anywhere regardless of whether he (the opponent) was in the same zone at the time the puck was passed or not (no "slow whistle").

(g)   **(For Adult male checking games)**
        If the Linesman shall have erred in calling an off-side pass infraction (regardless of whether either team is shorthanded), the puck shall be faced on the center ice face-off spot.

Rule 628 Puck Out of Bounds or Unplayable

(a)   When the puck goes outside the playing area or strikes any obstacles above the playing surface other than the boards, glass or wire, or deflects off an Official out of the playing area, it shall be faced-off from where it was shot or deflected by a player, unless otherwise expressly provided in these rules.
        If the puck leaves the playing area or becomes unplayable due to a defect in the playing rink, a face-off will take place at the point where the puck was last played.
        (b)   When the puck becomes lodged in the netting on the outside of either goal so as to make it unplayable, or if it is frozen between opposing players intentionally or otherwise, the Referee shall stop the play and face-off the puck at either of the adjacent face-off spots unless in the opinion of the Referee the stoppage was caused by a player of the attacking team, in which case the resulting face-off shall be conducted in the Neutral Zone.

(Note) This includes a stoppage of play caused by a player of the attacking team shooting the puck onto the back of the defending team's goal without any intervening action by the defending team.
        The defending team and/or the attacking team may play the puck off the net at any time. However, should the puck remain on the net for longer than three seconds, play shall

be stopped and the face-off shall take place on an end zone face-off spot except when the stoppage is caused by the attacking team, in which case the face-off shall take place on a face-off spot in the Neutral Zone. However, if the puck comes to rest on top of the goal frame or in the netting on top of the goal frame, play shall be stopped immediately.

(c)   A minor penalty shall be imposed on a goalkeeper who deliberately drops the puck on the goal netting to cause a stoppage of play.

(d)   If the puck comes to rest on top of the boards surrounding the playing area, it shall be considered to be in play and may be played legally by the hand or stick.

Rule 629 Puck Must Be Kept in Motion

(a)   The puck must at all times be kept in motion. Play shall not be stopped because the puck is frozen along the boards by two more opposing players, unless a player falls on or is knocked down onto the puck. If one player freezes the puck along the boards or if a player deliberately falls on the puck a minor penalty for delaying the game shall be assessed under Rule 609(e) or Rule 612(a).

(Note) Notwithstanding the above, the Referee may stop play along the boards if in his judgment allowing play to continue will lead to unnecessary contact surrounding the puck.

(b)   A minor penalty shall be imposed on any player including the goalkeeper who holds, freezes or plays the puck with his stick, skates or body along the boards in such a manner as to cause a stoppage of play.

(c)   A player beyond his Defending Zone shall not pass nor carry the puck backward into his Defending Zone for the purpose of delaying the game except when his team is below the on-ice numerical strength of the opponents. For an infringement of this rule, the face-off shall be at the nearest end face-off spot in the Defending Zone of the offending team.

Rule 630 Puck Out of Sight and Illegal Puck

(a) Should a scramble take place, or a player accidentally falls on the puck, and the puck is out of sight of the Referee, he shall immediately blow his whistle and stop the play. The puck shall then be "faced-off" at the point where the play was stopped, unless otherwise provided for in the rules.

(b) If, at any time while play is in progress, a puck other than the one officially in play shall appear on the playing surface, which interferes with the progress of the game, the play shall be stopped immediately.

Rule 631 Puck Striking Official

(a) Play shall not be stopped because the puck touches an Official anywhere on the rink.

Rule 632 Refusing to Start Play

(a) If, when both teams are on the ice, one team for any reason shall refuse to play when ordered to do so by the Referee, he shall warn the Captain and allow the team so refusing 15 seconds within which time to begin the game or resume play. If at the end of that time the team shall still refuse to play, the Referee shall impose a bench minor penalty on the offending team and the case shall be reported to the proper authorities for further action. Should there be a recurrence of the same incident, the Referee shall have no alternative but to suspend the game and impose a match penalty on the offending Team Official(s) responsible for the incident.

(b) If a team, when ordered to do so by an On-Ice Official, through a Team Official, fails to go onto the ice promptly, it shall receive a bench minor penalty. If the team fails to go onto the ice and start play within five minutes, the game shall be suspended and the offending Team Official(s) shall be assessed a match penalty.

(Note) The local governing body or Disciplinary Committee shall determine whether the suspended game shall be deemed completed, forfeited, resumed from the point of suspension or cancelled and shall issue instructions pertaining to records, etc.

Playing Rules

Rule 633 Slashing

(a)   A minor or a major penalty shall be imposed on any player who slashes or attempts to slash an opponent with his stick.

(b)   A major plus a game misconduct penalty shall be imposed on any player who injures an opponent by slashing.

(Note) Referees should penalize as "slashing" any player who swings his stick at any opposing player (whether in or out of range) without actually striking him or where a player on the pretext of playing the puck makes a wild swing at the puck with the object of intimidating an opponent.

(c)   Any player who swings his stick at another player in the course of any altercation shall be subject to a game misconduct or a match penalty.

(Note) The Referee shall impose the normal appropriate penalty provided in the other sections of this rule and shall, in addition, report to the proper authorities.

(d)   A minor penalty shall be imposed on any player who makes stick contact with an opposing goalkeeper while he is in his goal crease, who has covered or caught the puck, regardless of whether or not the Referee has stopped play.

Rule 634 Spearing

(a)   A major plus a game misconduct penalty shall be imposed on a player who spears or attempts to spear an opponent.

(Note 1) "Spearing" shall mean poking an opponent with the point of the stick blade while the stick is being carried with one hand or both hands.

(Note 2) "Attempt to spear" shall include all cases where a spearing gesture is made regardless of whether or not bodily contact is made.

(Note 3) Spearing may also be treated as Attempt to Injure or Deliberate Injury of Opponents under Rule 603.

Rule 635 Start of Game and Periods

(a)   The game shall be commenced at the time scheduled by a "face-off" at the center ice face-off spot and shall be renewed promptly at the conclusion of each intermission in the same manner.

No delay shall be permitted by reason of any ceremony, exhibition, demonstration or presentation unless consented to reasonably in advance by the visiting team.

(b)   Home teams shall have the choice of goals to defend at the start of the game except where both players' benches are on the same side of the rink, in which case the home team shall start the game defending the goal nearest its own bench. The teams shall change ends for each succeeding regular period.

If in the opinion of the Referee, conditions are more favorable to play at one end of the rink than the other, the Referee may equalize opportunities by having the teams change ends at the middle of one or all three regular and overtime periods, but not in only two regular periods. The Referee shall declare before the commencement of the game or period that this change is to be made, and the change shall take place at the exact midpoint of a period and not at a stoppage of play nearest that point.

(c)   During the pregame warm-up (which shall not exceed 20 minutes in duration) and before the commencement of play in any period, each team shall confine its activity to its own half of the rink.

(Note) Players shall not be permitted to come on the ice during a stoppage in play or at the end of the first and second periods for the purpose of warming-up. The Referee will report any violation of this rule to the proper authorities for disciplinary action.

(d)   Fifteen minutes before the time scheduled for the start of the game both teams shall vacate the ice and proceed to their dressing rooms while the ice is being resurfaced. Both teams shall be signaled by the Game Timekeeper to return to the ice together in time for the scheduled start of the game or period. It is recommended that, when both teams are to leave

Playing Rules

the ice through a common exit, the team whose players' bench is closer to the exit leave first. The home team should enter the ice surface first.

(Note) This section is intended as a guideline only. In Youth and Girls/Women games, no time is required between the warm-up and the start of the game, if mutually agreed upon by both teams.

(e) When a team fails to appear on the ice promptly without a proper justification, an On-Ice Official shall warn the team through a Team Official that it must enter the ice immediately. If the team fails to do so promptly, the Referee shall assess a bench minor penalty for Delay of the Game. (See also Rule 632, Refusing to Start Play.)

Rule 636 Throwing Stick

(a) When any player or Team Official of the defending team deliberately throws or shoots a stick or any part thereof or any other object at the puck in his Defending Zone, the Referee shall allow the play to be completed and if a goal is not scored, a penalty shot/optional minor shall be taken by the player designated by the Referee as the player fouled.

If, however, the goal being unattended and the attacking player having no defending player to pass and having a chance to score on an "open goal," a stick or part thereof or any other object is thrown or shot by any member of the defending team in or into its Defending Zone, thereby preventing an obvious and imminent goal, a goal shall be awarded to the attacking team.

(Note 1) If the Officials are unable to determine the person against whom the offense was made, the nonoffending team, through the Captain, shall designate a player on the ice at the time the offense was committed to take the shot.

(Note 2) For the purpose of this rule, an open goal is defined as one from which a goalkeeper has been removed for an additional attacking player.

(b)   A minor penalty shall be imposed on any player on the ice who throws his stick or any part thereof or any other object in the direction of the puck in any zone, except when such act has been penalized by a penalty shot or the awarding of a goal.

(Note) When a player discards the broken portion of a stick by tossing it to the side of the rink (and not over the boards) in such a way as will not interfere with play or an opposing player, no penalty shall be imposed for so doing.

(c)   A misconduct penalty shall be imposed on any player or goalkeeper who throws a stick or any part thereof outside the playing area.

   If the offense is committed in protest of an Official's decision, a game misconduct penalty shall be assessed to the offending player.

   A game misconduct penalty shall be imposed on any player or goalkeeper who deliberately throws a stick or any part thereof outside the playing area at or in the direction of any spectators.

Rule 637   Time of Match or Time-Outs

(a)   The maximum time allowed for a game shall be three 20-minute periods of actual play with a rest intermission between periods.

   Play shall be resumed promptly following each intermission upon the expiration of 15 minutes from the completion of play in the preceding period. A preliminary warning shall be given by the Game Timekeeper to the Officials and to both teams three minutes prior to the resumption of play in each period and the final warning shall be given in sufficient time to enable the teams to resume play promptly.

(Note) For the purpose of keeping the spectators informed as to the time remaining during intermissions, the Game Timekeeper will use the electric clock to record length of intermissions.

(b)   The team scoring the greater number of goals during the three periods shall be the winner and shall be credited with two points in the standings.

Playing Rules

(c)   In the intervals between periods, the ice surface shall be resurfaced unless mutually agreed to the contrary.

(d)   If any unusual delay occurs in the first or second periods, the Referee may order the next regular intermission to be taken immediately and the balance of the period will be completed on the resumption of play with the teams defending the same goals, after which the teams will change ends and resume play of the ensuing period without delay.

(e)   Each team shall be permitted to take one time-out of a one-minute duration during the game, which must be taken during a stoppage of play. If one team takes a time-out, the opposing team may exercise the rights of a time-out, including warming up a goalkeeper. Nonpenalized players and goalkeepers may proceed to their respective team bench during any time-out.

     A time-out must be requested prior to the conclusion of the line change procedure. A team that is requesting its time-out during the same stoppage of play as their opponent's time-out must make such request prior to the conclusion of the first time-out.

     When the time-out is used to warm up goalkeeper(s), no more than four (4) pucks per team shall be allowed on the ice.

     During a game that has a time curfew (see Glossary), no time-outs shall be permitted.

(f)   If, in the opinion of the Referee, playing conditions beyond the control of the Officials and game participants (such as ice conditions, broken glass or weather) become unsatisfactory during the course of the game, the game may be suspended.

Rule 638   Tied Games

(a)   If at the end of the three periods the score is tied, the following shall take place:

(1) A 5-minute rest period will be allowed.

(2) The teams shall not change ends.

(3) A 10-minute period shall be played.

(4) The game shall terminate upon a goal being scored and the team scoring declared the winner. If no goal is scored, the same procedure shall be repeated.

(b)   Any overtime period shall be considered part of the game and all unexpired penalties shall remain in force.

(c)   If either team declines to play in the necessary overtime period or periods, the game shall be declared a loss for that team.

(Note) Districts and Regions may make their own rules regarding overtime for games under their jurisdiction.

Rule 639 Tripping

(a)   A minor or major penalty shall be imposed on any player who shall place his stick, foot, arm, hand or elbow, or extends the leg (Leg Checking) from the front or from behind, in such a manner that it shall cause his opponent to trip or fall.

(Note 1) If, in the opinion of the Referee, a player is unquestionably hook-checking or poke checking the puck and obtains possession of it, thereby tripping the puck carrier, no penalty shall be imposed.

(Note 2) Accidental trips that occur simultaneously with or after a stoppage of play will not be penalized.

Any player who deliberately leaves his feet and contacts an opponent with any part of his body thereby causing the opponent to trip or fall shall be assessed a minor penalty (Clipping).

(Note 3) This rule does not apply to a player who has dropped to his knee(s) to block a shot.

(b)   A major penalty plus a game misconduct penalty shall be assessed to any player who injures an opponent as a result of a foul committed by tripping or leg checking.

(c)   When a player in control of the puck beyond the defending blue line, and having no other opponent to pass than the goalkeeper, is tripped or otherwise fouled from behind, thus preventing a reasonable scoring opportunity, a penalty shot/optional minor shall be awarded to the nonoffending team. Nevertheless, the Referee shall not stop the play until the attacking team has lost possession and control of the puck to the defending team.

(Note) The intention of this rule is to restore a reasonable scoring opportunity that has been lost by reason of a foul from behind when the foul is committed in the Neutral or Attacking Zones.

"Possession and control of the puck" (See Glossary) means the act of propelling the puck with a stick. If, while it is being propelled, the puck is touched by another player or his equipment or hits the goal or goes free, the player shall no longer be considered to be "in possession and control of the puck."

(d)   If, when the opposing goalkeeper has been removed from the ice, a player in control of the puck beyond the defending blue line is tripped or otherwise fouled with no opposition between him and the opposing goal, thus preventing an obvious and imminent scoring opportunity, the Referee shall immediately stop the play and award a goal to the attacking team.

Rule 640 Unnecessary Roughness (Roughing)

(a)   At the discretion of the Referee, a minor or double minor penalty may be imposed on any player deemed guilty of unnecessary roughness. Any action worthy of a major penalty under this subsection must be assessed under Rule 613 (Fisticuffs).

For a body checking infraction in a nonchecking classification, a minor or major penalty shall be assessed under this rule.

(Note 1) In the Youth 10-or-under/Squirt and below, and in all Girls/Women classifications, body-checking is prohibited and shall be penalized under this rule.

When a team that is registered in a noncheching age classification plays against a team that is registered in a checking age classification, body-checking shall be prohibited under this rule.

A local governing body or league may prohibit body checking in any age classification.

(Note 2) In all nonchecking age classifications, a penalty shall be assessed under this rule whenever a player impedes the movement of a puck-carrying opponent by pushing him with the hands or arms or deliberately contacting him with the shoulder, hip or any other part of the torso.

There are instances when considerable body contact between the puck carrier and an opponent may occur that should not be penalized, provided that there has been no overt hip, shoulder or arm contact to physically force the opponent off the puck. Likewise, there shall be no penalty assessed if the puck carrier unsuccessfully attempts to skate through too small an opening between the boards and a stationary opponent and a collision occurs, unless there has been an overt action to body check the puck carrier.

Deliberate body contact on the part of the puck carrier may also be penalized under this rule. In order for a body checking penalty to be assessed, enough contact must have occurred to impede the movements of the puck carrier. A penalty may never be assessed for an attempt to body check.

A major plus a game misconduct penalty shall be assessed to any player who injures an opponent by body checking in a nonchecking classification.

(b)   Except for Adult age classifications, a minor or major penalty shall be assessed under this rule for any avoidable body check to an opponent who does not have possession and control of the puck. (See Glossary.) If the opponent is injured from this check, a major plus a game misconduct penalty shall be assessed.

(c)   A minor or a major penalty, at the discretion of the Referee, shall be imposed on a player who makes physical contact with an opponent after the whistle has been blown if, in the opinion of the Referee, the player has had sufficient time after the whistle to avoid such contact. If the opponent is injured from this check, a major plus game misconduct penalty shall be assessed.

Playing Rules

APPENDIX I
SUMMARY OF PENALTIES

The following summary of penalties is intended for general application of the rules. Specific situations may require different applications. All referenced rules should be consulted for exact language.

Minor Penalty

Personal Fouls

601(a)	Unsportsmanlike Conduct
601(b)	Shooting puck after whistle
613(a)	Instigator of fisticuffs
613(f)	Players not going to bench after warning during altercation
618(a)	Holding
621(a)	Interference
611(d)	Face-off interference
621(b)	Interference by player on bench
621(c)	Interfering with goalkeeper in crease
625(d)	Leaving penalty bench prematurely
633(d)	Stick contact with goalkeeper
639(a)	Clipping (leaving feet)

Delay of Game, Player or Goalkeeper

602(a, c)	Adjusting clothing/equipment
609(a)	Batting/shooting puck out of rink
609(b)	Shooting puck out of rink
609(c)	Deliberate goal displacement
609(e)	Freezing puck along boards or net
609(f)	Goalkeeper intentionally stops play
609(g)	Continued improper face-off position
611(b)	Second face-off violation, same team
612(a, b)	Falling on puck
615(d)	Picking up puck from ice
629(b)	Freezing puck along boards

Goalkeeper Infractions

303(d)	Wearing illegal equipment
406(b)	Thrown stick during penalty shot
407(d)	Leaving crease area during altercation
407(e)	Participating in play across center line
605(c)	Going to bench for stick at stoppage
615(a)	Holding puck more than three seconds
615(b)	Piling up obstacles in front of goal
628(c)	Dropping puck onto goal netting

Stick and Equipment Violations

301(d)	Playing with an illegal stick
301(d)	Player playing with goalkeeper stick
301(f)	Playing with more than one stick
304(a)	Equipment not worn under uniform
304(a)	Playing without helmet/facemask
605(a)	Playing with a broken stick
605(b)	Receiving an illegal stick
613(f)	Dropping glove(s)/stick in altercation
636(b)	Throwing a stick (non-Penalty Shot)

Bench Minor Penalty

104(e)	Goalkeeper warm-up area
109(c)	Alcohol, tobacco, smoking on bench
203(b)	Roster addition during game
203(c)	Improper goalkeeper substitution
205(a)	Too many players on the ice
205(d, f)	Illegal entry from penalty bench
205(e, f)	Goalkeeper to bench at stoppage
206(d)	Injured/penalized player returns prematurely
301(d)	Stick measurement legal
307(c)	Equipment measurement (legal)
308(a)	Use of electronic devices
601(c1, h2)	Obscene, profane, abusive language on players' bench
601(c2, h3)	Article thrown onto ice from players' bench
601(h1)	Team Official bangs boards
601(h4)	Team Official inciting opponent
601(h5)	Nonphysical interference with Game Official from players' bench
609(d)	Continued incorrect players on ice
632(a)	Refusing to start play
632(b)	Refusing to go on ice

Minor or Double Minor Penalty

640(a)	Unnecessary roughness

Minor or Major

604(a)	Boarding
606 (a, b)	Charging
608(a)	Cross-Checking
610(a)	Elbowing/Kneeing

616(a)	Head Contact
617(a)	High-sticking
619(a)	Hooking
633(a)	Slashing
639(a)	Tripping/Leg checking
640(a)	Body-checking in no-check game
640(b)	Avoidable check
640(c)	Checking opponent after whistle
#-	Major plus Game Misconduct required if resulting in injury

Minor plus Misconduct or Major plus Game Misconduct
607(a)	Checking from behind

Major plus Game Misconduct
608(c)	Butt-ending
607(b)	Checking From Behind (head first)
613(a, c)	Fisticuffs
603(d)	Head-butting
618(b)	Holding/grabbing facemask
625(b)	Leaving Bench in Altercation
634(a)	Spearing
640(a)	Injuring by body check (nonchecking)

Minor, Double Minor or Major plus Game Misconduct
613(b, e)	Fisticuffs (retaliation)

Minor plus Misconduct Penalty
301(e)	Not surrendering stick for measurement

Minor plus Game Misconduct Penalty
613(f)	Drop glove(s)/stick, instigate altercation

Bench Minor or Game Misconduct or both
625(h)	Team Official on ice without permission

Major plus Game Misconduct or Match
623(a)	Kicking opponent

Match Penalty
601(g1, j1)	Injury or attempting to injure Game Official
601(g2, j2)	Injury or attempting to injure opponent (except player to player)
601(g3, j3)	Detrimental behavior

603(a)	Attempt to injure opponent
603(a)	Deliberate injury of opponent
603(b)	Attempt to injure nonplayer
603(b)	Deliberate injury to nonplayer
603(c)	Taped hand, cutting opponent
632(a,b)	Suspended game—refusal to start play

Misconduct Penalty

304(b)	Helmet/facemask not worn on bench
304(c)	Mouthpiece violation
304(e)	Protective equipment violation
305(b)	Playing with cut palm on glove
406(f)	Distraction during penalty shot
601(a)	Persisting in unsportsmanlike conduct
601(d1)	Obscene, profane, abusive language (player)
601(d2)	Puck shot away from Official retrieving it
601(d3)	Throwing equipment out of rink
601(d4)	Not proceeding to penalty bench or dressing room
601(d5)	Player in Referee's crease
601(d6)	Nonphysical interference with Official

Game Misconduct Penalty

403(b)	Second major penalty in same game
404(d)	Five penalties to same player in game
601(a)	Persisting in unsportsmanlike conduct
601(f2, i1)	Obscene gesture (player or Team Official)
601(f2, i1)	Racial/ethnic slur
601(f1)	Persisting player conduct, after Misconduct
601(i2)	Persisting Team Official conduct, after Bench Minor
601(i3)	Physically interfering with Game Official
613(d)	First to intervene in altercation
622(b)	Player interference with spectator

Misconduct or Game Misconduct Penalty

601(e1)	Touching or holding Game Official
601(e2)	Continuing altercation after warning
601(e3)	Banging boards or glass with stick (player)
636(c)	Stick thrown out of playing area

Game Misconduct or Match Penalty

| 633(c) | Swinging stick at opponent in altercation |

enalty Shot (only)

205(c)	Deliberate illegal substitution
609(c)	Goalkeeper deliberately displaces goal, no break-away
609(c)	Deliberate removal of helmet/facemask, break-away
621(f)	Thrown stick, break-away
625(g)	Illegal entry, break-away

enalty Shot or Awarded Goal

609(c)	Deliberate goal displacement in scoring opportunity
612(c)	Player falling on puck in crease
615(d)	Player picking up puck from crease
636(a)	Stick thrown at puck in Defending Zone
639(c, d)	Fouled from behind on break-away

warded Goal (only)

609(c)	Deliberate goal displacement preventing a goal
615(b)	Goalkeeper stick left in front of goal, preventing a goal

APPENDIX II
SUMMARY OF
FACE-OFF LOCATIONS

Center Ice Spot

635(a)	Start of game and periods
611(i)	Goal scored
205(b)	Premature goalkeeper substitution (normal)
627(g)	Offside pass error by officials

Neutral Zone Spot

409(b)	Coincident icing and delayed penalty
611(f)	Stoppage by attacking player in Attacking Zone
611(f)	Attacking player shoots puck onto netting
611(f)	Gathering of players
621(d)	Goal crease violation
626(b)	Puck carried off-side
626(g)	Off-side error by officials
628(b)	Attacking team makes puck unplayable

End Zone Face-Off Spot

406(g)	Unsuccessful penalty shot attempt
611(h)	Last play face-off between end spots and end boards
611(i)	Goal illegally scored off official
615(c)	Goalkeeper throws puck forward
617(a)	Slap shot, 10-or-under and younger
617(d)	High-sticked puck
620(a)	Icing
620(g)	Icing error by officials
626(e)	Intentional off-side
628(b)	Defending player shoots puck onto netting
629(c)	Bringing puck back into Defending Zone

Last Play Face-Off

611(g)	General rule
205(b)	Premature goalkeeper substitution (exception)
409(a)	Penalty on team in possession
409(b)	Stoppage following delayed penalty signal
611(g)	Fouls by players on both sides simultaneously
615(e)	Hand pass
622(a, c)	Interference by spectators
625(k)	Off-side player entering from players' bench
626(b)	Puck passed off-side
627(a)	Center line off-side pass
628(a)	Puck strikes overhead obstruction/rink defect
629(a)	Stalled puck between opposing players
630(a)	Puck out of sight of Referee

APPENDIX III
OFFICIAL SIGNALS

BOARDING

Striking the closed fist of the hand once into the open palm of the other hand.

BODY CHECKING (NON CHECKING CLASSIFICATIONS)

The palm of the nonwhistle hand is brought across the body and placed on the opposite shoulder.

BUTT-ENDING

Moving the forearm, fist closed, under the forearm of the other hand held palm down.

CHARGING

Rotating clenched fists around one another in front of chest.

CHECKING FROM BEHIND

Arm placed behind the back, elbow bent, forearm parallel to the ice surface.

CROSS-CHECKING

A forward motion with both fists clenched, extending from the chest.

DELAYED CALLING OF PENALTY

The nonwhistle hand is extended straight above the head.

DELAYED WHISTLE (SLOW WHISTLE)

(Blue-Line Off-Sides, Adults only)
The nonwhistle hand is extended straight above head. If play returns to Neutral Zone without stoppage, or as soon as the offending team clears the zone, the arm is drawn down.

DELAYING THE GAME

The nonwhistle hand, palm open, is placed across the chest and then fully extended directly in front of the body.

ELBOWING

Tapping the elbow with the opposite hand.

FIGHTING (ROUGHING)

One punching motion to the side with the arm extending from the shoulder.

GOAL SCORED

A single point, with the nonwhistle hand, directly at the goal in which the puck legally entered, while simultaneously blowing the whistle.

HAND PASS

The nonwhistle hand (open hand) and arm are placed straight down alongside the body and swung forward and up once in an underhand motion.

HEAD CONTACT

Nonwhistle hand placed palm inward on the back of the helmet.

HIGH-STICKING

Holding both fists clenched, one immediately above the other, at the side of the head.

HOLDING

Clasping the wrist of the whistle hand well in front of the chest.

HOLDING THE FACEMASK

Closed fist held in front of face, palm in and pulled down in one straight motion.

HOOKING

A tugging motion with both arms, as if pulling something toward the stomach.

ICING

When the puck is shot or deflected in such a manner as to produce a possible icing situation, the back linesman will signal to his partner by raising his nonwhistle hand over his head (same as Slow Whistle). The instant that the conditions required to establish "icing the puck" have occurred, the front linesman will blow his whistle to stop play and raise his nonwhistle hand (same as Slow Whistle). The back linesman will give the icing signal by folding his arms across his chest.

INTERFERENCE

Crossed arms stationary in front of chest with fists closed.

KNEEING

A single tap of the right knee with the right hand, keeping both skates on the ice.

MATCH PENALTY

Pat flat of hand on top of the head.

MISCONDUCT

Placing of both hands on hips one time.

PENALTY SHOT

Arms crossed (fists clenched) above head.

SLASHING

One chop of the hand across the straightened forearm of the other hand.

SPEARING

A single jabbing motion with both hands together, thrust forward from in front of the chest, then dropping hands to the side.

TIME-OUT OR UNSPORTSMANLIKE CONDUCT

Using both hands to form a "T."

TRIPPING

Strike the side of the knee and follow through once, keeping the head up and both skates on the ice.

"WASHOUT"

Both arms swung laterally across the body at shoulder level with palms down.

1. When used by the Referee, it means no goal or violation so play shall continue.

2. When used by the Linesmen, it means there is no icing, off-side, hand pass or high sticking violation.

APPENDIX IV
OFFICIAL RINK DIAGRAMS

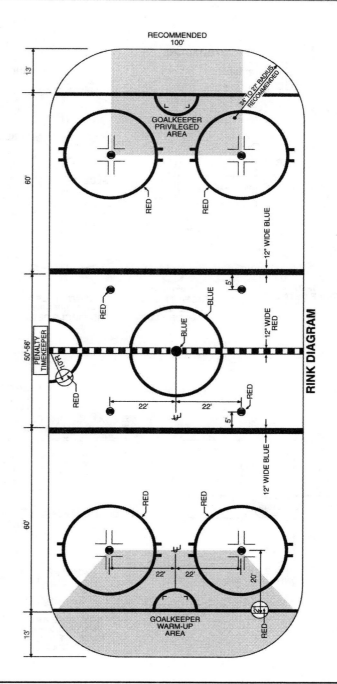

RECOMMENDED
100'

13'

24" TO 27" RADIUS
RECOMMENDED

GOALKEEPER
PRIVILEGED
AREA

60'

RED

RED

12" WIDE BLUE

5'

RED

BLUE

BLUE

BLUE

12" WIDE
RED

50'-56'

PENALTY
TIMEKEEPER

10'R

RED

22'   22'

RED

5'

RED

RINK DIAGRAM

12" WIDE BLUE

RED

RED

60'

22'   22'

20'

RED

GOALKEEPER
WARM-UP
AREA

13'

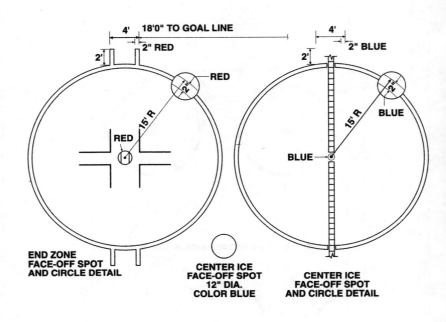

END ZONE FACE-OFF SPOT AND CIRCLE DETAIL

CENTER ICE FACE-OFF SPOT 12" DIA. COLOR BLUE

CENTER ICE FACE-OFF SPOT AND CIRCLE DETAIL

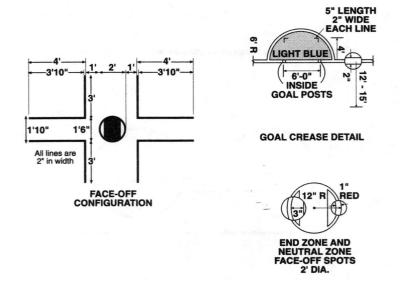

FACE-OFF CONFIGURATION

All lines are 2" in width

GOAL CREASE DETAIL

5" LENGTH 2" WIDE EACH LINE

LIGHT BLUE

6'-0" INSIDE GOAL POSTS

END ZONE AND NEUTRAL ZONE FACE-OFF SPOTS 2' DIA.

APPENDIX V
GLOSSARY

Age Classifications

The following Youth and Girls/Women age classifications have been established for all teams registered with USA Hockey.

Youth Teams: 8-or-under (Mite), 10-or-under (Squirt), 12-or-under (Pee Wee), 14-or-under (Bantam), 16-or-under (Midget) and 18-or-under (Midget).

Girls/Women Teams: 8-or-under, 10-or-under, 12-or-under, 14-or-under, 16-or-under and 19-or-under.

(Note 1) Girls/Women playing on a Youth team must conform to the Youth age classification.

(Note 2) High School age classification is governed under the same playing rules as the Youth 18-or-under (Midget) age classification.

(Note 3) Adult classifications shall include Adult noncheck, Adult U.S., Adult Elite and Adult Women, and shall be governed by these rules, except where otherwise noted.

Altercation

Any physical interaction between two or more opposing players resulting in a penalty or penalties being assessed.

Body Checking

A legal body check is one in which a player checks an opponent who is in possession of the puck, by using his hip or body from the front, diagonally from the front or straight from the side, and does not take more than two fast steps in executing the check.

Legitimate body checking must be done only with the trunk of the body (hips and shoulders) and must be above the opponent's knees and below the neck. If body checking is unnecessarily rough, it must be penalized.

Body Contact

Contact that occurs between opponents during the normal process of playing the puck, provided there has been no overt hip, shoulder or arm contact to physically force the opponent off of the puck.

Break-away

A condition whereby a player is in control of the puck with no opposition between the player and the opposing goal, with a reasonable scoring opportunity.

Butt-Ending

The condition whereby a player uses the shaft of the stick above the upper hand to jab or attempt to jab an opposing player.

Coach

A Coach is a person primarily responsible for directing and guiding the play of his team. Along with the Manager, he is responsible for the conduct of his team's players before, during and after a game.

Coincident Penalty

A penalty of equal type (e.g., minor or major) assessed during the same stoppage of play, and for which neither team is reduced in on-ice numerical strength. A coincident penalty never causes either team to be "shorthanded" for purposes of penalty termination if a goal is scored.

Creases

Goalkeeper's-Areas marked on the ice in front of each goal designed to protect the goalkeepers from interference by attacking players.

Referee's-Area marked on the ice in front of the Penalty Timekeeper's seat for the use of the Referee.

Cross-Checking

When a player, holding his stick with both hands, checks an opponent by using the shaft of the stick with no part of the stick on the ice.

Delayed Off-Side

A situation where an attacking player has preceded the puck across the attacking blue line, but the defending team has gained possession of the puck and is in a position to bring the puck out of their Defending Zone without any delay or contact with an attacking player.

Deflecting the Puck

The action of the puck contacting any person or object, causing it to change direction.

Directing the Puck

The act of intentionally moving or positioning the body, skate or stick so as to change the course of the puck in a desired direction.

Face-Off

The action of an official dropping the puck between the sticks of two opposing players to start play. A face-off begins when the Referee indicates its location and the officials take their appropriate positions, and ends when the puck has been legally dropped.

Fisticuffs

The actual throwing of a punch (closed fist) by a player that makes contact with an opponent.

Game Suspension(s)

When a player, Coach or Manager receives a game suspension(s), he shall not be eligible to participate in the next game(s) that was already on the schedule of his team at the time of the incident.

Goalkeeper

A goalkeeper is a person designated as such by a team who is permitted special equipment and privileges to prevent the puck from entering the goal.

Head-Butting

The physical use of one's head in the course of delivering a body-check (head first) in the chest, head, neck or back area or the physical use of the head to strike an opponent.

Head Contact

The action of a player intentionally or recklessly contacting a player in the head, including with the stick or by an illegal body check (as defined in this Glossary).

HECC

The Hockey Equipment Certification Council is an independent organization responsible for the development, evaluation and testing of performance standards for protective ice hockey equipment. To date, there are standards for facemasks, helmets and skate blades.

Heel of the Stick

The point where the shaft of the stick and the bottom of the blade meet.

Hooking

The action of applying the blade of the stick to any part of an opponent's body or stick and impeding his progress by a pulling or tugging motion with the stick.

Injury Potential Penalties

Injury Potential Penalties include Butt-Ending, Checking from Behind, Head-Butting, Spearing, Board Checking, Charging, Cross Checking, Elbowing/ Kneeing, High Sticking, Holding the Facemask, Slashing and Roughing. The Linesman may report such infractions to the Referee, following the next stoppage of play, that have occurred behind the play and were unobserved by the Referee.

Last Play Face-Off

The location at which the puck was last legally played by a player or goalkeeper immediately prior to a stoppage of play.

Off-Ice (Minor) Official

Officials appointed to assist in the conduct of the game including the Official Scorer, Game Timekeeper, Penalty Timekeeper and the two Goal Judges. The Referee has general supervision of the game and full control of all game officials, and in case of any dispute the Referee's decision shall be final.

Penalty

A penalty is the result of an infraction of the rules by a player or team official. It usually involves the removal from the game of the offending player or team official for a specified period of time. In some cases the penalty may be the awarding of a penalty shot on goal or the actual awarding of a goal.

Player

Member of a team physically participating in a game. The goalkeeper is considered a player except where special rules specify otherwise.

Possession of the Puck

The last player or goalkeeper to make contact with the puck. This includes a puck that is deflected off a player or any part of his equipment.

Possession and Control of the Puck

The last player or goalkeeper to make contact with the puck and who is also propelling the puck in a desired direction.

Proper Authorities (Proper Disciplinary Authority)

The governing body of the team or teams involved, as determined by the Affiliate, except:

(1) In USA Hockey Tournaments and Play-Offs, the body shall be the Discipline Committee of the Tournament or Play-Off.

(2) In matters relating to assault of official, the body shall be the Affiliate Association of that team.

Protective Equipment

Equipment worn by players for the sole purpose of protection from injury. Recommended equipment should be commercially manufactured.

Shorthanded

Shorthanded means that a team is below the numerical strength of its opponents on the ice. When a goal is scored against a shorthanded team, the minor or bench minor penalty that terminates automatically is the first such noncoincident penalty (the minor or bench minor penalty then being served with the least amout of time remaining). Thus, if an equal number of players from each team is serving a penalty(s) (minor, bench minor, major or match only), neither team is "shorthanded."

Slashing

The action of striking or attempting to strike an opponent with a stick or of swinging a stick at an opponent with no contact being made. Tapping an opponent's stick is not considered slashing.

Spearing

The action of poking or attempting to poke an opponent with the tip of the blade of the stick while holding the stick with one or both hands.

Substitute Goalkeeper

A designated goalkeeper on the Official Scoresheet who is not then participating in the game.

Team Official

A Team Official is any person on the players' bench who is not on the game scoresheet as an eligible player or goalkeeper. All such persons must be registered in the current season as a Coach with USA Hockey, and must have attained the appropriate certification level as required by the District and/or Affiliate. One such person must be designated as the Head Coach. A player or goalkeeper on the roster who is unable to play, other than through suspension, may be on the players' bench without being considered a Team Official if he is wearing the team jersey and all required head and face protective equipment.

Temporary Goalkeeper

A player not designated as a goalkeeper on the Official Scoresheet who assumes that position when no designated goalkeeper is able to participate in the game. He is governed by goalkeeper privileges and limitations and must return as a "player" when a designated goalkeeper becomes available to participate in the game.

Time-Out (Curfew definition)

A curfew game is one in which the game must end by a certain time of day. Conversely, a noncurfew game is one that will be played to clock time conclusion, regardless of how long the game lasts.

APPENDIX VI
RULE REFERENCES

NOTES

NOTES

NOTES

NOTES

NOTES

NOTES

NOTES